Praise for

GET AHEAD OF PROPAGANDISTS

"A must read to expose and defuse disinformation."

– Nancy Snow, lead author of the 8th edition of *Propaganda and Persuasion* (Sage, 2025)

"Very good analysis. Jacques Ellul himself, along with his lifelong friend, Bernard Charbonneau, also believed in forming groups to discuss media propaganda."

– Randal Marlin, author *Propaganda and the Ethics of Persuasion*

"Brilliant–a strong call to action based in solid research!"

– Kay Sprinkel Grace

"I've enjoyed reading Rodney Miller's blog posts for a number of years, particularly those focused on contemporary problems of propaganda. Rodney's posts on propaganda, now collected and thematized, lay out a hopeful blueprint for commentators and teachers who aim to diagnose and alleviate obstacles to clear thinking and thoughtful communicating."

– J. Michael Sproule, author *Democratic Vernaculars: Rhetorics of Reading, Writing, Speaking, and Criticism since the Enlightenment*

"This is interesting, comprehensive, and well researched. With the mayhem of discourse that surrounds us now in the 21st century, I would like to hear real debates on ideas."

– Patsy McCarthy, coauthor *Speaking Persuasively*

"I enjoyed this commentary on propaganda. It's spot-on!"

– Lisa Bennett

GET AHEAD OF PROPAGANDISTS

Rodney G. Miller's critically acclaimed writing includes his book on persuasive language styles–named Reviewer's Choice by senior reviewer at Midwest Book Review, Diane Donovan. He is published by the State University of New York Press and The Royal Society of Queensland. His popular blog shares insights on accountable communication at:

communicator.rodney-miller.com

BY RODNEY G. MILLER

Bestest Words
Communication Essays
Communication & Beyond
Australians Speak Out: Persuasive Language Styles
Get Ahead of Propagandists: Countering Disinformation

Get Ahead of Propagandists

Get Ahead of Propagandists

Countering Disinformation

Rodney G. Miller

Parula Press

PLEASE NOTE

The blog posts in this book were first published at the author's website: communicator.rodney-miller.com and are republished here for educational, reference, or other personal use. The book supplements collected blog posts with a bibliography and an index.

Cataloging-in-Publication Data
Name: Miller, Rodney G., author
Title: *Get Ahead of Propagandists: Countering Disinformation*
Description: Albany, NY: Parula Press, [2024] / Rodney G. Miller; Includes notes, bibliography, index
Subjects: LCSH: 1. Communication – Media Studies 2. Propaganda – Disinformation 3. Politics and Government – Democracy

ISBN: 978-1-7374895-7-3 (ebook)
ISBN: 978-1-7374895-3-5 (paperback)

Library of Congress Control Number: 2022904642

For "the free inquiring, critical spirit"[1]

– Sinclair Lewis, *It Can't Happen Here*, 1935

Terminology

Conspiracy Theories – "variety of thinking patterns that are known to be unreliable tools for tracking reality...not supported by evidence that withstands scrutiny."[2]

Disinformation – "deliberate dissemination of information that is false, with the express aim to mislead or obfuscate."[3]

Fake News – "false stories that appear to be news, spread on the internet or using other media, usually created to influence political views or as a joke"[4] ...also now a highly political term often used as a buzzword.[5]

Microtargeting – online use of personality profiles for "relentless targeting that plays 'to the fears and the prejudices of people, in order to alter their voting plans.'"[6]

Misinformation – dissemination of false information that unintentionally misleads or obfuscates.[7]

Propaganda – "organized attempt through communication to affect belief or action or inculcate attitudes in a large audience in ways that circumvent or suppress an individual's adequately informed, rational, reflective judgment."[8]

Pseudo-populism – political approach that advances *anti*-democracy to oppose alleged "elites" on behalf of "the people." Some classifications associate populism with *anti*-democratic politics.[9]

Table of Contents

Introduction

We have it in our power to begin the world over again.[10]

– Thomas Paine, *Common Sense*, 1776

When *Common Sense* was first published, it was read aloud in taverns and meeting places. This was in the emotion-charged time of early 1776, prior to the signing of the Declaration of Independence. Some in the yet to be United States were ambivalent about whether to "reconcile" with England. The pamphlet is impassioned and powerful, though not an easy read in certain passages for a modern reader.

It remains one of the best-selling publications in the United States. The then anonymous author Thomas Paine noted in a postscript to the Introduction that his identity was "wholly unnecessary... [except] ...That he is unconnected with any Party, and under no sort of Influence public or private, but the influence of reason and principle."[11]

Paine advocates specific steps for needed action, drawing on both intuition and reason. Many of his comments remain pertinent. Take, for example, his conclusion: "Let the names of Whig and Tory be extinct; and let not other be heard among us, than those of a GOOD CITIZEN, AN OPEN AND RESOLUTE FRIEND, AND A VIRTUOUS SUPPORTER OF THE RIGHTS OF [HU]MANKIND AND OF THE FREE AND INDEPENDANT [sic] STATES OF AMERICA."[12]

Centrally, the pamphlet makes a powerful condemnation of autocracy, specifically targeted at the King of England. But the key criticisms pertain to autocrats anywhere, anytime. Common to autocrats, then and now, is insatiable self-interest. And like any empty vessel, an autocrat will make the most noise, propping up partisan posturing to divert attention from real concerns.

If you'd like to push back on the meandering nonsense autocrats use to intimidate and control, there are some thoughtful guides available. One is the book *How to Stand Up to a Dictator*[13] by Maria Ressa, who was awarded the Nobel Peace Prize, at least partly in recognition of her effective efforts to stand up to then President Duterte in the Philippines.

The book exposes the underbelly of intimidation typically employed by autocrats against individuals who advocate basic freedoms. Most valuably, Ressa provides a compelling recap on her lessons learned, along with steps that she and her team take to fight back and survive. Much of what she describes to deal with autocracy's weaponization of the news, social media, the law, and education is applicable to efforts needed worldwide to strengthen democracy.

The book brings together personal and professional understandings. Ressa shapes workable wisdoms from life experiences to guide her actions. She describes a desire early in life, "...to know myself to such a degree that I could take myself out of the equation when approaching the world around me and responding to it. That is clarity—the ability to remove your self and your ego."[14] Just some lessons distilled from her professional experiences are "...we couldn't stay quiet because silence is consent. ...don't let anyone else tell your story...,"[15] or "Free speech is being used to stifle free speech,"[16] or "Every day of inaction is a day of injustice...,"[17] or "My hope is that others can replicate our three pillars: technology, journalism, and community to fight back and build forward."[18]

And she details how to uncover and address autocrats' manipulation of social media, sharing plans and the actions she takes to check if not checkmate a dictator. More than interesting and compelling, Ressa outlines much to put into action.

She doesn't only detail how social media use us. She also outlines how anyone determined to strengthen democracy can, with some planning, support, and savvy, turn social media against the *pseudo-populist* actions of autocrats. On this point, she advises that, "If your nation has elections coming up, organize your #FactsFirst pyramid a year earlier. The very minimum is six months."[19] Ressa describes how to do this. Hers is a unique and transferrable story of how to "...*fight for our future.*"[20] Not easy, but very doable by people committed to do the work needed to assure a better future.

Another book–an even more personal guide–is the widely-known *On Tyranny* by Timothy Snyder. He draws on the rear-vision-mirror of history, to anticipate and tackle the ruinous rants of contemporary tyrants in our midst. While revealing the reality behind the masks that tyrants use, Snyder's major contribution in this simple and short work is to offer twenty useful actions. These are his distillations of "...*twenty lessons from the twentieth century,*"[21] to help keep perspective and be prepared.

From his initial advice not to obey in advance, through some down-to-earth personal suggestions for preserving truth, to getting prepared to deal with the worst outcomes, he provides a pocket-guide to deal with deniers of freedom. Some samples are "Power wants your body softening in your chair and your emotions dissipating on the screen. Get outside,"[22] or "Be angry about the treacherous use of patriotic vocabulary,"[23] or "Set a good example of what America means for the generations to come. They will need it."[24] By eating away at democratic freedoms, autocrat-propagandists undermine the democratic system in unsubtle ways–sapping everyone's energy and initiative.

For anyone who cares about strengthening democracy, these publications and any others that are as clear about needed actions are worth checking out. You can expect them to be more use than the repetitive outrages amplified by social media and mass media, or the morass of stories focusing on grifters, crime, and violence that dominate video entertainment and so-called news.

In both democratic and autocratic states, too many harmful propagandists hold sway. Despite frequent warnings, people mostly go about daily life paying little attention to how much various forms of propaganda do harm. Ignoring or excusing insults, outrage, screeches for the camera, or other verbal and nonverbal abuse grants power to bullies, trolls, wannabe tyrants and terrorists, whether online or face-to-face.

Propagandists will tell us what we want to hear to secure this power. The gold standard of effective propaganda for an autocrat-propagandist is to wrap together into daily "news" disinformation, misinformation, conspiracy theories, fake news, and *pseudo-populist* appeals, eventually fully engaging people in the propagandist's worldview.

This is a fantasy world that wraps mundane, daily realities in the propagandists' preposterous imaginings. It is a conglomerate of fantasy and reality. When enough of our family, friends, neighbors, workmates, and others accept this worldview, the autocrat-propagandist secures and continuously strengthens the desired control of large numbers of people.

But being bathed with sensation-seeking, polemical echoes from empty vessels has limits. As Nancy Snow observes, "It is up to individuals with a strong vision that includes a wider lens on the world to move us from the pseudo-reality of what is to a better world of what may be."[25]

1: Are We Ready?

Without Freedom Of Thought There Can Be No Such Thing
As Wisdom & No Such Thing As Publick Liberty Without
Freedom of Speech[26]

– Benjamin Franklin, 1722

During 2024, many nations are holding elections for heads of state, national/state representatives, or referenda including more than the 60 nations on this List of elections worldwide in 2024[27]–with some electors, more than others, truly able to strengthen democracy.

As Albert Camus astutely observes, "the best case for democracy is what it prevents."[28] As far back as the eighteenth century, it was shown mathematically that:

> ...collectively, members of a group who have imperfect but above-chance information about competing alternatives are more likely to choose the "correct" alternative than any one member of the group.[29]

Reassuring perhaps, yet worldwide in many places and especially in the United States, we are witnessing a long-term trend of generational decline in support for democracy.[30] This decline is at least partly fueled by strategic disinformation that undermines belief in evidence-informed policy making[31]–to disrupt the operation of democracy.

On any day, voters will need to navigate a firehose[32] of propaganda that wraps together the imperatives of fake news, disinformation, misinformation, conspiracy theories, and *pseudo-populism*. Each burst of verbiage, image, or deed[33] is designed to grab attention, resonate, and stir people to action.

The Big Challenges

People worldwide who value democratic freedoms are faced with detecting and dismantling this propaganda. For democracy to thrive, some larger converging trends require attention.

- Burgeoning computerized propaganda systems.[34]
- Government impotence regulating social media platforms—perhaps we can expect similar failures regulating anticipated hazards of Artificial Intelligence.
- Ever-increasing pressure in social media and mass media to help grow audiences by amplifying what is outrageous.

These largely unchecked trends are having intensified effects on us. Propagandists continuously use the capabilities of computer networks, social media, and mass media powerfully against democracy.

To strengthen democratic society and reassert law and civility, each of us must find ways to deal with some urgent questions of our time: Why do people accept obvious lies? Why do family, friends, or neighbors continue to support propagandists attacking democracy? When and how should you call out the nonsense and outrageous talk of the farcical public figures, who belong elsewhere than the public stage? Why are the weaknesses of propaganda not more substantially worked on?

As individual citizens, we are mostly on our own to tackle the harms of propaganda. If you would like a future where democracy is more than a footnote within a history book (which won't be allowed on the school library shelf), best get prepared for the wilds of no-debate land—a Wild West where governing norms are anachronisms, like the rancher's open range and pitiful imitations of the Marlboro Man.[35]

Institutions and People

Institutions do not themselves protect democracy. Montesquieu suggests the durability of free government depends on a nation's self-correction.[36] Meanwhile, bad actors exploit the snail-paced, incremental processes of legislators, judiciary, and others occupying responsible roles. Promptly holding bad actors to account is what matters. This will often require taking steps well beyond any established zones of comfort within institutions, professions, or job descriptions.

But propagandists are generally more talked about than accountable. It is well past time to expect our legislators, judiciary, and others in responsible roles to be fully effective doing their jobs, to ensure our well-being. What we say and do now matters to demand accountability.

It is more than urgent for each of us to find better ways to require better. And to find ever-stronger ways to engage the talent, creativity, and drive of new generations to do the same.

This book offers some ways to deal with propaganda. It is not about all propaganda, which many thoughtful commentators seek to describe.[37] The book explores how propaganda works, as well as ways to: block, blunt, or counter its effects; enlist the media in this effort; extend education for countering propaganda; and push to criminalize egregiously harmful lies of propagandists.

The surprise, outrage, scandal, repetition, novelty, rumor, fervor, or occasional humor built into a propagandist's words, soundbites, memes, or actions appear direct, simple, or even simplistic. But however foolish we might initially believe some nonsense to be, its repetitive occurrence, including our own verbatim repetitions, too quickly cause great harm to individual freedoms and democracy.

Better Future

It is perfectly reasonable to expect elected representatives to increase protections to assure personal liberties, security, physical safety, freedom from violence or threats of violence, freedom from censorship, the right to vote in free and fair elections, and true protection of the integrity of electoral processes.

This is no time for nattering about elected or wannabe autocrats, or to be swamped by microanalyses of their diversions. Amid the news reports and endless books published that review democratic decay in the United States, a nagging concern is that even the best of these do little more than uncover malign activity–with some putting a laser focus on diagnosis. Most fail to offer much remedy. Workable steps to outwit propagandists are hard to come by. Mostly, journalists and pundits keep revealing disasters that continue like cancer to eat away at the democratic system in unsubtle ways.

No time either for writing extended instructions and elaborate action plans. Countering current propaganda ahead of the next continuous stream of drivel is what matters. We need to develop better ways to:

1) Hold propagandists to account.

2) Block and counter propaganda continuously.

3) Strengthen capabilities and freedom of the mass media.

4) Expand systematic education on countering propaganda.

5) Push for regulation against the harms that propagandists cause.

6) Foster collaborative groups sustaining these efforts.

We face one of the most critical periods of history, in which, more than ever, vigorous efforts are required to block, blunt, and counter the propaganda that undermines democratic freedoms. It is time to effectively tackle ongoing threats to personal security and democratic government.

Cooperative Efforts

Deciding whether or how to respond to a propagandist firstly requires quick but careful assessment of what potential harm might occur from the propaganda. When an audience is small or the negative impact modest, most distortions, ambiguities, or even lies potentially damaging to an individual or democratic values, policies, or processes might be best ignored.

Frequently, the most effective approach to handling a propagandist is to respond with plain talk–just telling the truth, preferably with humor, without quixotically tilting at the propagandist's fantasies. It is simple, direct truth that hurts the propagandist most–other than being ignored of course!

In cooperation with or alongside legislative, judicial, and media efforts, we can all help to make a difference by building ways to blunt, block, and dismantle propaganda.

Urgent and long overdue are better focused individual and collaborative actions. We need to go beyond just revealing or diagnosing daily disasters of largely unchecked wannabe-autocrats. Critiques of propaganda must be laser focused to detect and dismantle the effects and consequences of its so-called content.

Creativity and commitment from all of us–especially the more thoughtful members of the mass media as well as individuals who will start or join coalitions for action–are now needed to find ways to succeed against those who erode democracy.

2: Can We Stop Whistling in the Wind?

... propaganda only seems to succeed when it coincides with
what people are inclined to do in any case.[38]

– George Orwell, 1944

Propagandists are largely parasitic. A parasite lives and feeds on or in
another organism of another species, causing harm to its host. As if we
are another species,[39] propagandists exploit us as they obsess with self-
advancement. More than offensive or demeaning, continuous streams of
manufactured, outrageous talk cause serious harm. We delude ourselves
by paying too little attention to the extent of the harm done to us.

Great Harm

Most obviously, much political propaganda now incites hate, violence,
or government overthrow. Propagandists routinely use fear, vanity, greed,
or other basic emotions to cause social divisions and chaos, or damage to
reputation, along with individual and larger scale fraud in financial, health,
or electoral decision-making. Propaganda is a much used cover-up of
corrupt practices or behavior in institutions, harming individuals within
or outside an institution.

10

Viewed through the lens of the parasite analogy, the propagandist draws on our culture, beliefs, and emotions to weaken the quality of life that we value. These agents of Newspeak[40] are so present that friends, family, and neighbors tire of hearing about them in the media or just about anywhere else.

In the United States, mass media have frequently broadcast entire political rallies of a candidate, again and again and again, for months on end. This was acknowledged at the time by the occasional broadcast media executive as not good for America, but "damn good" for the broadcaster.[41]

Entranced with fourth-rate celebrity, if that's all that's available, many in the mass media still regurgitate trite outrage or worn-out quotable quotes as *breaking news*. Perhaps it's a pious wish that broadcasters will ever recognize that many of us have had enough rehashes of the latest doings of a propagandist being paraded before us. Many of us are continuing our shift to streaming platforms.

Is There Good Propaganda?

Propaganda is not new. But it is not well understood. Some folks sincerely suggest there is good propaganda. One widely available definition of propaganda considers it as "helping or injuring ...deliberately to further one's cause or to damage an opposing cause."[42] According to this view, propaganda might advance whatever is either negative or positive.

Propaganda principles, processes, and techniques certainly seem agnostic to political or moral positions or "-isms." But the reality is that any propaganda is fully effective when the independent will and the capacity for choice by "targeted" individuals are denied. Can a propagandist with good intent somehow purify propaganda when pursuing a common good?[43] Both good and bad actors use propaganda processes to secure their results by creating "pseudo-needs."[44]

Commonly these days, political propagandists sow chaos, confusion, and false crises to exploit our limited attention to the consequences of what they say and do. The French philosopher Jacques Ellul explains in his landmark study that propaganda is an ongoing process constantly shaping expectations through:

> ...continuous agitation... [creating] ...a climate first, and then prevent[ing] the individual from noticing a particular propaganda operation in contrast to daily events.[45]

Ironically and sadly, our own preoccupation with what we call propaganda helps ensure that public policies or action to address the real needs and wants of people take a back seat to the endless microanalyses of the propagandist–or are simply ignored. Propagandists confidently rely on daily regurgitation of their public talk in news reports, social media, and elsewhere. This control of the public agenda significantly reframes our thinking.

Even as we disdain spin merchants, they tell us what we want to hear, wrapped in cultural myths that pander to our deepest feelings. Savvy propagandists are adept at incorporating myths in this way, frequently promising a better future. And what people believe about the future is what shapes response to present events.[46]

Images of a lifestyle or a national identity might be valuable for an individual or for social cohesion, but propagandists value such beliefs in us as tools of control.

What Is Propaganda?

Understandings of the word *propaganda* range widely, including from what someone disagrees with[47] through to puffery or hyperbole for promotion. Whether or not we like a cause, product, or person promoted can affect what we call propaganda, or what we feel about a propagandist's claim.[48]

Even reaching agreement among scholars on a useful definition of the word[49] remains difficult. Some efforts seek to distinguish rhetoric, persuasion, and propaganda based on whether intentions are revealed or hidden, how much interaction or participation seems possible, whether

12

discourse is truthful,[50] or whether rational decision-making is respected. A definition that Garth S. Jowett and Victoria O'Donnell offer focuses on the purpose of propaganda:

> Propaganda is the deliberate, systematic attempt to shape perceptions, manipulate cognitions, and direct behavior to achieve a response that furthers the desired intent of the propagandist.[51]

Control of Thought

Alone or in collusion with collaborators, propagandists continuously attack both free thought and, by extension, freedoms of speech and association. Ellul observes "to be effective, propaganda must constantly short-circuit all thought and decision."[52] He alerts to propaganda being "a menace that threatens the total personality,"[53] warning that any fully effective propaganda provokes "action without prior thought."[54] And this "action makes propaganda's effect irreversible."[55]

Once we are sufficiently prepared to make automatic response, we the propagandized increasingly give ourselves over to what the propagandist says about everyday events. Commercial, political, and cult-promoting propagandists all seek automatic response[56] to further their interests. Seriously examining propaganda requires a definition that embraces this driving effect.

After reviewing a wide variety of definitions, Randal Marlin offers a workably clear description, which is the framework stipulated here:

> PROPAGANDA = The organized attempt through communication to affect belief or action or inculcate attitudes in a large audience in ways that circumvent or suppress an individual's adequately informed, rational, reflective judgment.[57]

This aptly infers that a propagandist's effectiveness depends on the extent to which audiences surrender free choice. This most substantial harm to individuals and society is not easily addressed. Such commandeering of people's thinking and actions continuously corrupts the freedoms on which democracy is based. As will be explored later, the processes of

13

propaganda and democracy are at odds,[58] through the impact on each of us and on democratic processes.

Although propaganda has an inevitable presence in society and can serve to unify the beliefs of a community, talking about "harmful propaganda,"[59] as if there is any that is not, should not sit well with anyone committed to freedom.

Not to Be Fooled

Continuous immersion in nonsense wrapped in deeply felt myths really messes with otherwise sensible pundits, politicians, academics, and each of us. In daily life, we all accept bursts of verbiage, image, or deeds designed to grab our attention washing over us from an early age.

Even before we reach teen years, the electronic babysitter of television delivers countless, unfiltered stimulations of dopamine in the brain. Its effects are much like a narcotic causing addiction. This engagement helps tech platforms soon afterwards to fulfill their goal for more of us to spend more time on social media.

Are we whistling in the wind to expect civic leaders, neighbors, friends, family, or any of us to outwit propagandists? Productively unmasking propagandists or redirecting their efforts requires some agreement about what's going on.

Ellul suggests that the "endless repetition of formulas, explanations, and simple stimuli" erodes "scorn and disbelief."[60] However foolish we might initially believe some nonsense to be, its repetitive use focuses both conversation and actions. Accordingly, the most educated, intelligent people in the community remain the most propagandized because each–

* Absorbs the largest amount of second-hand information.

* Feels compelled to have an opinion

* Takes pride in thinking clearly and "judging."[61]

Thanks to George Orwell's short essay "Politics and the English Language," we can be more alert to public figures who use words to obscure or deliberately hide realities. Orwell tried to help with simple advice to catch and push back on language that is "designed to make lies sound truthful and murder respectable."[62] Together with his description of Newspeak in the novel *Nineteen Eighty-Four*,[63] we have an early warning and basic ways to deal with this verbal abuse.

Orwell also presented us with a further warning about the consequence and effect of a propagandist's language distortions. His fairy story *Animal Farm*[64] darkly illustrates how autocratic pigs take over the farm. They use the other animals' fuzziness of memory and limited reasoning ability to confuse collective memories about previous practices and norms.

The pigs secure obedience to their new regime largely because their fellow animals continuously ponder ambiguities, without taking any action. Through this failure, the animals give permission in advance[65] to cede control of the farm to the pigs, increasing the speed with which all are controlled.[66]

The most effective antidotes to propaganda remain truth and the ability to distinguish "fact from opinion and the proven from the plausible"[67]–to differentiate the light from the dark and the many shades between.

.

3: Understanding Propaganda

...the continual effort and alarm attendant on a state of continual danger will compel nations the most attached to liberty to resort for repose and security to institutions which have a tendency to destroy their civil and political rights. To be safe... [people] ...at length become willing to run the risk of being less free.[68]

– Alexander Hamilton, 1787

What Alexander Hamilton observes about the debilitating effect of continuous chaos in war also applies to how we are targeted in the propaganda war. Manufactured outrage is a weapon in the war on democracy. Aspiring autocrats worldwide copy-cat mirages of chaos, calamity, or carnage. Their fake news, disinformation, misinformation, and conspiracy conjectures use *pseudo-populist* appeals to construct a disturbing kaleidoscope.

The frequently discordant or contradictory claims acquire consistency by resonating with what we value in the presuppositions of society.[69] Ellul names the persistence of some myths, such as nation, youth, hero, work, and the belief in progress. These myths "evoke the future."[70] He suggests

16

propagandists tap into such myths to help drive automatic behavior by a social force that deprives us of our core being.[71]

How We "Hear" Propaganda

Even though presuppositions of a society may be expressed in myths, metaphors, or national narratives, these are not necessarily uniformly understood by people. Different people perceive different connotations in words and phrases—and may differently assign denotation in what we "hear."

Our point of view is central to how we understand propaganda. It's no more than a convenient illusion to think and act as if meaning is fixed in a word, phrase, image, or action and that everyone uniformly "gets it," much less that they should, or that it is the same *it*. Exposing what any propaganda means requires more than restating some meme or slogan, as if there is a single discoverable meaning that we all uniformly get.

As the linguist Noam Chomsky remarks "communication is a more-or-less matter, seeking a fair estimate of what the other person said and has in mind."[72] David Sless and Ruth Shrensky point out that we each perceive words, images, music, actions, or events etc. differently—with each of us playing "...an active part in the making of the meaning."[73] They offer that signs have meaning that we project onto them, suggesting we make meaning by projecting our "prior knowledge...seamlessly."[74]

While Sless and Shrensky do recognize public language or common meaning, they observe that generally "it's hard to decide what may be shared."[75] Authentic analysis of propaganda will appreciate there are a wide variety of points of view in audiences, with many contexts in play to influence understanding or action.

Aligning Meanings

Acknowledging that each of us brings different projections and accommodations to what we perceive requires that we change how to think about communication and therefore how to interpret propaganda. Additionally, a specialty of propagandists is to assert certainties while stimulating ambiguity. Savvy propagandists are especially adept at infecting their public discourse with words of certainty and ambiguity that resonate with myths or presuppositions.

News reports were not so long ago infiltrated with words like *celebrity president, fake news, deep state, tremendous success,* or many others. Such verbal combinations claim attention and touch off presuppositions. Each spotlights the propagandist's own perspective and is designed to elicit desired responses in us. The term *semantic infiltration* was coined by Fred Iklé to describe the use for which these words are designed:

> Simply put, semantic infiltration is the process whereby we come to adopt the language of our adversaries in describing political reality.[76]

When we repeat such words, we assist the propagandist's efforts. And we encourage others to do the same. The mass media assist the propagandist's efforts by headlining much of this word-salad in reports of current events. This is complicated further by propagandists infiltrating false dichotomies, narrow-casting, or otherwise reframing words we commonly use, most notably *freedom* and *democracy.* At worst, we can become megaphones for the propagandist's worldview, to reach audiences well beyond what the propagandist might accomplish unassisted.[77]

Claims and Ambiguities

It is many repetitions, especially with variation, that powerfully reinforce. For example, in the United States all the way to January 6 of 2021 and beyond, all media persistently regurgitated verbatim propagandist slogans like "Stop the Steal"–which disseminated insurrectionist claims widely. Whether or not media reports are perceived as neutral or slanted positively or negatively, the continuous repetition of this verbiage reinforces the propagandist's "certainties." So much repetition of rants and ramblings inevitably increases their significance.

The repeated parroting of a big lie, even though we might oppose the claims of a propagandist, should be viewed as one form of advancing permission to control the public agenda, as well as our lives.[78] And such claims land resoundingly in the disinformation land of the suburbs, where feelings of safety and security may be easily disturbed. In many countries, it's here that elections are often decided.

Journalists, pundits, and social media users continuously take the bait of propagandists' outlandish claims and name-calling. They even respond in kind, with characterizations of a propagandist as "bully," "infantile," "racist," or "unhinged." Persistent repetition of even what's grossly negative about a propagandist will nonetheless help advance the propagandist's name, identity, and style.

On the flip side, a propagandist can benefit when words are so over-used that they no longer register with us. For example, it's likely that after a time the frequent repetition of a propagandist's threats to destroy democracy may become meaningless to listeners—like a weird version of Aesop's tale about the Boy Who Cried Wolf. Meanwhile, these repetitions serve the dual role of providing the media hungry propagandist with additional coverage through the propagandist's own follow-up denial of the media's parroting.

We see decay already in the meaning of words for which the use-by dates are well passed, thanks largely to their frequent occurrence in the mass media—like "existential," "untruth," and "unprecedented." This process is analogous to what's known as *semantic satiation.* Although psychology researchers still debate how the process occurs, high repetition appears to cause a word or phrase to temporarily lose meaning for a listener.[79]

And a savvy propagandist will also powerfully exploit varieties of ambiguity among the certainties. Marlin describes how the ambiguity of some verbs or nouns can promote intention. For example, the ordinarily positive verb *help* accentuates a negative intention in the sentence "James helped John lose." Marlin illustrates how the use of such verbs as "brought about" or "ensured" or "engineered" may impute an intention that the "doer" did not have. He elaborates how "a skillful propagandist can exploit this kind of ambiguity," by implying an intention to bring about a consequence.[80]

19

Within the continuous drumbeat of invented conspiracies, ambiguity is common too. Philip Collins notes this in the frequently propagated supposed conspiracy of some unnamed elite against people, which claims "utopia [is] just around the corner, if only the corrupt elite had cared to venture there." He points out the propagandist's self-portrayal as leading efforts to "rise above the smears, and ludicrous slanders from ludicrous reporters."[81] Yet another example is the classic *bandwagon* device "a lot of people are saying," used as authority for some preposterous drivel. With a zealot's energy, such a propagandist will launch attacks on "enemies" and other "vermin."

Preoccupied with self-advancement, by any means, at the expense of anyone else, propagandists routinely talk in authoritative-sounding imperatives to assert their often outrageous claims. They distract from reality, denying, destabilizing, and destroying our established norms, values, and even the operation of valued institutions.

How Propaganda Works

But it can be difficult at times to challenge what propagandists say, since they so often deal in ill-defined extremes. They stimulate uncertainty about core values, leaving confusion—even encouraging a belief that it is others who are propagandized.

Linguists will tell us propagandists use imperatives heavily and a high proportion of vacuous content words with unclear referents. They use lots of function words to add ambiguity or emphasize extremes—like factive verbs and non-referential adverbs.[82] A propagandist's exaggerations include of course playing on the fear of *other* groups in society, or pandering to deep-seated desires... for recognition, for virility, for accomplishment, or for belonging, for example.

Because audience members perceive certainties and ambiguities differently, the propagandist can tap into a range of perceptions. Perhaps this helps with negotiating feelings of proximity[83] with a wide array of "propagandees," including among people with widely varying beliefs. It seems there are as many different propaganda as members of a large audience. Now there's a challenge for quantitative research!

The dynamic processes of propaganda are akin to how rumor works. As people project personal concerns into a rumor, this modifies and spreads it widely. Propagandists likewise fuel their reach through novelty, contrariness, exaggeration, and ambiguity resonant with our presuppositions. As Ellul noted about the empowering effect in rumor:

> ...the farther away the source and the greater the number of individuals who have passed it on, ...the more the objective fact loses importance and the more the rumor is believed by the multitudes who adhere to it.[84]

And propaganda distributed digitally, or even through mass media, will morph at least as readily and widely as village gossip. In addition to ease of dissemination, these media deliver on the prime purpose of propaganda to cause audience action.[85] Digital communications offer many options to engage audiences in using these media to further the propagandist's interests and chain these "doers" to the propagandist.

While propaganda is sometimes described as a top-down approach seeking exclusive control of all communication channels, a wide range of accessible media available today negates the need for control of all communication channels for propaganda to succeed. Grassroots or multi-headed campaigns in sympathy with each other need not align exactly for a propagandist to dominate the thought of others sufficiently to incite action—which makes especially urgent the need to neutralize this propaganda.

4: Neutralize Propaganda

Propaganda ceases where simple dialogue begins.[86]

– Jacques Ellul, 1962

In 2022 in the United States, during a break in the televised Congressional Hearings to probe the attempted overthrow of democratic government, a thoughtful media commentator asked why we hadn't seen "all this" as it took shape. Despite the substantial disinformation and other propaganda distractions leading up to and after the attack on the Capitol, tens of millions of Americans might answer that thanks largely to media coverage, they long sensed the illicit behaviors. And turned out in very large numbers to vote in 2020, and subsequently, to reassert democracy.

Anyone listening during the previous half decade or more had already detected the clear and imminent danger of overt public attacks on democracy. Early red flags were public polemic to discredit the FBI and the media, along with assaults on democratic norms, the rule of law, and the institutions of democracy. Many voters recognized these were neither subtle nor random attacks. For many, the Congressional Hearings just added some detail on how a coup was hatched.

22

Election workers, whistleblowers, local officials, judges, attorneys, journalists, and many more showed resilience against threats, violence, and character assassination, enabling voters to speak out. Enough voters who identify as Independent or Republican joined with Democrats to bolster democracy–offering hope for some reprieve from a dark alternative. Less clear is how long this coalition of voters will withstand the ongoing menace of mutating propaganda.

Where We Are Now

This is a time to be clear-eyed about the mirages that propaganda creates. Repelling all the propaganda washing over us may not be possible. With thoughtful action though, we can detect and deflect much of its impact. Suggested below and following in later chapters are some ways to block, blunt, or counter fake news, disinformation, misinformation, conspiracy conjectures, *pseudo-populism,* and propaganda more broadly.

The most thoughtful media commentators ignore or paraphrase a propagandist's catchy words, slogans, and other noise. Some substitute "criminal defendant" or another factual descriptor, instead of using a propagandist's name for a second or further times. These commentators spotlight the actions rather than the words of a propagandist, or illustrate the likely harmful effect from doing what the propagandist urges.

Inferring the realities of the harm inherent in what a propagandist advocates is ordinarily straightforward. Likewise, to point out the propagandist's failure to offer any real solutions to benefit us. It's best to address how the claims in propaganda or the actions of propagandists would impact us. Other helpfully neutralizing narratives are to use the power of analogy, especially to illustrate the resilience and creative resourcefulness of people standing up to tyranny. These can include stories locally, from elsewhere, or from earlier times. Shared successes dealing with *anti*-democratic propaganda[87] both build resilience and stimulate additional individual or collaborative push back.

It's essential NOT to amplify the name, claims, and antics of a propagandist. The power of personality politics makes it even more important to minimize promotion of a propagandist's name or words, even when these are widely known and promoted by others.

Yet this basic electioneering wisdom is too little observed. Obsessions with micro-analyzing a propagandist's supposed intentions, or excessive mockery, or focusing only on so-called secrets,[88] lies, or ideology in propaganda tend not to wash with audiences beyond the "party faithful." The most effective propaganda uses truth and focuses on "mundane issues, not ideological appeals."[89]

Likewise, it's best not to place too much faith in recurring verbal attacks on a propagandist, given the mixed results from the intense attacks of this type in election campaigns. As will be noted later, although judicious and penetrating illustration of how the graft harms voters directly may be helpful to deflect propaganda, the United States, as well as some other nations, too often elect accused criminals to public office—despite vigorous commentary on the candidate's alleged criminality.

Most importantly, all of us need to reclaim the public agenda, so that we oblige action on matters important to everyday living. We can all call out and push back on nonsense talk with well-targeted rhetorical or direct questions that require attention to what matters to voters—such as common concerns about healthcare, jobs, shelter, food, safety, freedom, and holding bad actors to account.

Fortunately, the continuous immersion in sensation-seeking echoes from empty vessels does have some limits. In someone substantially reshaped by propaganda, a small boost of propaganda will readily excite or "re-intoxicate" a person.[90] But mostly, for people not mingling in the propagandist's world and worldview, propaganda is not very durable.[91] A wonderful quality of propaganda is how quickly it decays when crowded out of public discourse, without opportunity for a "refresh." As mentioned previously, there's not much that a propagandist fears more than being ignored.[92]

Engaging Conversations

Three principles offer hope for neutralizing propaganda: (1) conversation one-on-one or in one-on-two groups can evolve coalitions among even the most polarized individuals;[93] (2) likewise effective is to keep focus on addressing the consequences and effects of a propagandist's claims or actions, with little or no direct reference to the propagandist by name; and (3) propaganda decays when denied opportunity for a "refresh."

Very effective talk-show hosts, pundits, and journalists exemplify the first principle, with a talent for sustaining a conversational tone to "interact" with the theoretical average of two-and-a-half people listening in any living room, workplace, vehicle, or elsewhere. These professionals help many keep perspective, sometimes by offering creative insights for dealing with propaganda designed to polarize and to undermine democracy.

One television anchor recently described how a town's civic leaders in Colorado systematically engaged the polarized residents through one-on-one or one-on-two discussions. These folks then built cooperative efforts to benefit the community–after "town halls" and even small group meetings were found not to work. Unsurprisingly, one of the more effective civic leaders in this effort was the town's fire chief.[94] Especially in an election year, strategically extending such initiatives for community action are crucial. This approach builds on the remarkable commitment to volunteerism in the United States.[95]

Simple dialogue will engage individuals within a community to stand together to meet day-to-day or emergency needs–delivering real solutions, in contrast to a propagandist's puffery. Autocrat-propagandists primarily use polemic of *dispute,* which is concerned with winning. This polemic allows for no mutually accepted procedure to find solutions. While the processes of two other types of polemic, namely, *discussion* and *controversy,* enable resolution of differences, the only remedies for handling *dispute* polemic are punishment, therapy, or disregard.[96]

Autocrat-propagandists erode the consultative decision-making that makes democracy work. To counter polarization, what is more important than engaging a propagandist's "targets" productively in community decision-making?

Probing the effects or consequences of propagandists' disinformation, rather than repeating it, can also be fruitful for investigative journalists, or anyone with interest in follow-through. For example, one potential news item concerns a study that estimated the effect of propagandists who advocated the use of hydroxychloroquine (HCQ) during the first wave of COVID-19.

A meta-analysis of randomized trials shows that HCQ use was associated with an 11% increase in mortality rate among some patient groups, with the number of hydroxychloroquine related deaths in hospitalized patients estimated at 16,990 in six countries during just a two-year period.[97] Continuously revealing the likely or actual effects or consequences of a propagandist's claims can help illustrate the dangerous or vacuous character of propaganda.

Whistleblowing

It will often be an investigative journalist who blows the whistle on the bad actions of a propagandist. But, for any real impact, these efforts require dogged follow-up questions and critiques. Frankly, some of us at least expect the media to uncover and track initiatives and proposals from politicians that would improve everyday living. Or, when no proposals are offered, to give repeated access to credible voices urging initiatives that could work. Or, to require politicians to make more than mealy-mouthed promises, as well as to require accountability, repeatedly as needed, for delivery on promised initiatives.

Media probes that advocate more timely and effective use of the legal system against the harmful actions of propagandists may also help strengthen democracy. Largely through persistently professional media investigations is much malfeasance of elected or aspiring officials ever known. And journalists deploy information gathering and writing abilities within standards of the profession, media management, perceived audience interests, and other constraints that would paralyze many people.

The regularity of discovering and getting to us what might be truly "fit to print" or broadcast is an ever-changing landscape, ever demanding on talent, patience, persistence, politeness, and a host of other positive human qualities. On the flip side, too many in the mass media industry fail to dial back naive or worse amplifications of manufactured outrage–and dialing back coverage of the propagandist's harmful nonsense is essential to reassert civility!

Among continuing attempts to encourage the news media toward practices better than reactionary sensation-seeking are initiatives commenced around 2015 to disseminate the practices of constructive journalism.[98] The approach of constructive news is "to find practical solutions to the challenges which face its audience, forcing politicians to make evidence-based proposals, which one could then evaluate over time, pegging their words back to reality…"[99] Let's wish for journalism schools and, increasingly, practicing journalists to devote considerable effort to constructive news practices or similar.

Early detection and pre-emptive actions are especially critical to neutralizing propaganda. Democracies generally move too slowly to require accountability of propagandists–even with demonstrably bad actors, who aggregate personal power by gaming the laws and procedures designed to sustain democracy. The sad lesson of history is that wannabe autocrats move with relative speed to exploit democratic freedoms.

These characters steal the march on us with screeches for the camera and relentless fundraising. They use large-scale, systematic psychographic profiling to micro-target very large numbers of people. Unimpeded, fundraising emails, social media, advertising spots on the Internet, and other outputs rally supporters and bait opponents into wasteful, reactionary responses. Character assassination of a political opponent and other outlandish claims are commonplace.

The failure to push back effectively on propagandists for many months or years continuously empowers the most accomplished. Prompt accountability for illegal behavior is required to reassert truth, law, and justice.

Limits of Propaganda

Specific clues for what propaganda to tackle most vigorously, as well as how to do so, are found in what Ellul concludes as some limits of propaganda in his time. He suggests that propaganda: (1) can only very slowly modify pre-existing attitudes; (2) cannot successfully deny general social trends or the strong sociological factors on which society acts; (3) must be consonant with some basic fact; (4) must be lasting and continuous to sustain psychological impact; and (5) when delivered by a foreign nation may be limited by the propagandist's limited awareness of the target nation's attitudes, centers of interest, and presuppositions.[100]

Actions anyone can take against a continuous propaganda onslaught are to:

1. Challenge any propaganda that targets our pre-existing attitudes on which democracy is based. We can do this as basically as through reassertion of core values, like honesty, justice, prudence, courage, and wisdom.

2. Highlight the harm to people that would result from the claims of any bad actor—saying exactly what should happen instead. And push civic leaders to promptly hold bad actors accountable.

3. Reassert the rightness of facts, positively, briefly, and specifically, without naming the lie or the liar—to avoid becoming a megaphone for the corrupt.

4. Keep advocating and repeating our desire to live in a society that enables the provision of basic human needs, such as health, job, shelter, food, safety, and freedom. This directly counters the vacuous claims of propaganda, which decay over time—especially when crowded out of public communications.

5. Push for legal and financial sanctions to hold accountable both foreign propagandists and their collaborating domestic dupes, who undermine our way of life with threats, hacks, hoaxes, fraud, or other harms.

Propagandists will only side-step the limits of propaganda when we let them, including by allowing our energy to be diverted, such as by over-reacting to their drivel. Most vital to neutralizing propagandists is for each of us to keep perspective and build ways to tackle propaganda wherever it is useful to do so—with speed, frequency, pertinence, and reach.

It is practical expressions of truth, law, and justice that ensure democracy thrives, by fending off the incursions of bad actors, both domestic and foreign. Speaking up and speaking out to elected and aspiring officials, the judiciary, the media, and anyone who will listen is needed to strengthen democracy. Democracy greatly depends on our continuous attention, thought, and action to continue and thrive.

5: Counter *Anti*-democracy

Things would be better if people took an interest in local politics...[101]

– Bertrand Russell, 1952

Democratic societies have a spotty record of containing or sufficiently dealing with the propaganda that autocrats and aspiring autocrats use, especially domestically. Yet, united worldwide through invisible links stronger than titanium are people who want to live in a genuine democracy. Regardless of local or national differences, we agree on the value of freedom.

Fully effective propaganda degrades and then destroys the freedoms needed for the participation and cooperation that are foundations of democratic societies. Propaganda perverts the public agenda—especially since it "has always been understood to involve *bribes* and *threats of physical coercion* as well as linguistic-based deceptions."[102] But the aberrant outrage or deeds that local dupes parrot from their autocratic, foreign collaborators appear oddly in the "silly seasons" of continuous electioneering—and are readily deflected through prebunking.

Some government responses, especially to foreign propaganda, can be very effective. For example, prior to the invasion of Ukraine in 2022, the early and repeated release of declassified military intelligence by the United States had real value[103] to blunt the propaganda that came soon after from the invader. The declassified intelligence set a context for people globally to understand the invasion, the war itself, and the propaganda of the invader. And this provided context on a well-documented, so-called "strongman"[104] who obtained and sustains power through pre-emptive bluff, persuasion, and intimidation.

Speaking Out

Our speaking up freely and well offers the simple dialogue required to advance the common good. Anything less is just lip-service to democracy. Ellul foreshadows that propaganda in a society paying lip-service to a democratic creed creates a people who are suited to a totalitarian society, because they cling to clear certainties.[105] Yet the respect for freedoms of thought, speech, and association in liberal democracies opens many pathways for those seeking to deny freedoms–enabling grifters, charlatans, pretenders, and others to compete alongside the genuine to increasingly undermine the values, laws, practices, norms, or other guardrails of democracy.

For example, so-called populism in the United States inclines "towards anti-democratic ends."[106] For now, the blueprint for destroying checks and balances on power and abusing political power is to deploy formally legal procedures to pervert the Constitution and other laws, undermine elections, and delay accountability–while trying to give an impression that "nothing illegal is going on...[maintaining]...a veneer of democracy and legality."[107]

Norms of politeness, civility, or other values present in a democracy too often inhibit the media, elected representatives, and many citizens from even calling a lie what it is. Ellul observes that propaganda suppresses "...liberal democracy, after which we are no longer dealing with votes or the people's sovereignty."[108] Consequently, liberal governments are confronted with the dilemma that using propaganda to deal with propaganda can erode the basis of democratic government. As Marlin notes, Ellul pointed out the need for:

31

...liberal government to offset seditious ideas from within the state or... [use] ...propaganda to offset other states seeking conquest over one's own state. But he recognizes that once a state begins to engage seriously in propaganda, it erodes its own claim to being liberal.[109]

Reputable outlines of propaganda warn of this inherent danger, regardless of whether the propagandist's purpose is to "injure" or to "further" a cause, and regardless of whether the cause is for a common good. At times though, democratic leaders appear frozen and overly concerned about potential for backlash to take needed action.

Legacies of Control

The challenge to sustain independent thought and actions against a propagandist is not new. Propaganda is "present in human history as early as the formation of the first states."[110] From the earliest recorded uses, propaganda has helped autocrats to "convince subordinates of their connection to gods and local mythologies."[111] Through ancient Mesopotamian, Egyptian, and Mayan civilizations, visual propaganda is recorded. Alexander the Great (356 BC - 323 BC) "is considered...an ancient master of propaganda."[112] He was long thought to be the first to see propaganda as a powerful way to reinforce "cohesion and control" over people and to continuously reinforce "just where the center of power resided."[113]

Likewise in ancient Rome, for more than a decade Augustus (63 BC - AD 14) consolidated his rule largely free from conflict as first emperor, in part by self-promoting and boosting his following via a wide range of propaganda, including literature, statues, monuments, and coins. Until the close of the eighteenth century, autocrats sustained a long period of *anti*-democratic rule globally through coercion and propaganda.

To Sustain Democracy

In the twentieth century, an explosion in mass media amplified the effectiveness of the propaganda of dictators, who engineered the fall of modern democracies through two world wars and continuous conflicts since. These events stimulated efforts to understand and deal with propaganda. In the 1930s in the United States, with:

> ...the global rise of fascist regimes who were beaming propaganda across the world...scholars and journalists were struggling to understand how people could fall for lies and overblown rhetoric.[114]

With the founding of the United States at the close of the eighteenth century, its Constitution established a Republic governed by freely elected representatives of the people. Its people are committed through The First Amendment to protect freedoms of speech, religion, press, assembly, and petition to the Government for redress of grievances. Americans construe "the term democracy as a shorthand for *liberal democracy*," apparently finding consistency in definition at least.[115]

Yet democracy itself will always remain a contested concept.[116] The scale of modern government, the roles of party whips or lobbyists, the growth of bureaucracy, and continuous media amplification of propaganda all challenge how "individual citizens can make their voices heard."[117] Noam Chomsky is hardly alone in believing that a:

> truly democratic community is one in which the general public has the opportunity for meaningful and constructive participation in the formation of social policy: in their own immediate community, in the workplace, and in the society at large.[118]

Independent people will push back against false promises or any threats to freedoms.

Being First

Propaganda efforts commence long before most people realize. Drawing on people's cultural values and social assumptions, the propagandist first conditions us with a long period of *pre-propaganda*.[119] This involves months or more of patient activity. In this phase, the propagandist might be barely noticed at first, stepping into occasional news of daily events–building a presence and increasing a following.

During this time, the propagandist's commentary will ordinarily be contrarian in praise or correction of selected people, events, or initiatives. Sometimes, early signs of being under the sway of a foreign "strongman" will occur, such as by making an odd response publicly to a softball question from a foreign adversary's representative. But the more bizarre the commentary, the more it is amplified in the media. Unchallenged, these efforts gradually establish so-called *new thinking*. The effect is to stimulate reappraisal of individual or social values and norms.[120] A stream of contrarian commentary increases perception of a propagandist as an "influencer" whom followers look to.

This long *pre-propaganda* phase enhances name-recognition, gathers followers, and starts to frame the public agenda, while establishing habits in the media to falsely amplify the significance of the propagandist. Failure to push back in this phase makes resistance ever more problematic. Prejudices strengthened in people in the absence of prebunking or debunking[121] are very resistant to change. Regrettably, by the time any effective response is made, if at all, much damage is done. Whether during initial efforts or later, pre-emptive detection and dismantling of what's going on is vital.

Typical "Tells"

A propagandist attacking democracy is easily detected when you know what to look for. Some personal features, not often noted, are the valuable "tells" described by Collins.[122] He observes in Adolf Hitler's speaking and propaganda some features that are eerily present in the manner and language of today's demagogues. The "signature emotion of a Hitler speech is anger," with "tells" that he was, in his own words, "accustomed to strike back at any attacker" and firmly believed "that leniency will not succeed in appeasing."[123] At a closer language level, Hitler often claimed that no one compared to himself had "done as much... in the service of..."[124] some cause.

Another common "tell" of autocrats is self-indulging how poorly-done-by they and their followers are, especially by the media not loving them—with autocrats seeming to be forever angry.[125] And their utopia ordinarily requires returning to a mythically better past; apparently unable to show us a better future, much less to do so with humor. When such "tells" occur repeatedly, these can serve as red flags to signal both the presence and the obsessions of an autocrat. Apparently, this is all in every day's "work" for this self-dealing person.

Agitation and Integration

The transition from the *pre-propaganda* phase mobilizes propaganda of *agitation and integration*[126] to carry efforts forward. To disrupt and destabilize our comfort with norms that we value, a propagandist might bleat claims about supposed social ills causing "carnage" or foretell an apparently endless variety of apocalyptic futures.

Within these agitation efforts, or soon afterwards, it's inferred or asserted that the imagined ills can only be remedied by the propagandist— if only those listening will align with the propagandist! Increasingly, threats of violence amplify illusions of power. And the ordinarily unchallenged presumption of power delays accountability, denying the effectiveness of the legal procedures required to sustain democratic government. This also enables public displays of supposed victimhood, with which a base of supporters readily identifies—touching off their further "intoxication" through echoes of earlier propaganda claims.

Memes, aphorisms, platitudes, or catch cries are intensified to megaphone the supposed "values" of the propagandist, or seek unity against a presumed enemy, or promote the idyllic value of a some never delivered utopia. Over time, countless combinations of *tough* and *sweet* talk[127] will cajole or comfort, tapping basic desires or wants in people. Ellul also describes both *vertical*, top-down propaganda of a leader, as well as *horizontal propaganda* which is used inside a large group or organization of people.[128] He details how different types of propaganda function, including *rational* and *irrational propaganda*.[129] In Ellul's time at least, propaganda that is disconnected from facts or is "violent, excessive, shock-provoking" was ultimately less convincing to stimulate participation.[130]

35

It's often best just to assume such a propagandist is a weird person, driven by self-interest to develop skills in self-preservation from probably a very early age via a distorted commitment to being right and trying to win at everything—by whatever means—including into adult life through threats, bluff, and remarkably protracted gaming of the legal system. The continuous propaganda is largely targeted to reinforce the beliefs of supporters, appeal to potential swing voters, and bait opponents. These are three priorities to counter vigorously.

Dismantle *Anti*-democracy

It is important to counter *anti*-democratic discourse that erodes key truths of democratic society, or blocks free thought, speech, and association, or that people find threatening. Domestic and foreign bad actors routinely advance mutually reinforcing disinformation that contaminates public debates to promote "hateful narratives...Existing conflicts in society may be artificially increased in order to destabilise the society"[131] to a level that constitutes a security threat.

Direct action individually and collectively must tackle the *anti*-democratic playbook of commentary and actions. Well understood among proponents of *anti*-democracy are ways to:

- Erode key truths of democratic society.
- Block free thought, speech, and association.
- Threaten coercion against advocates of democracy.

Individually or in small groups face-to-face or online, it is vital to scrutinize a propagandist's actions or claims. Detecting and dismantling this propaganda demands tough-mindedness, together with keeping touch with what's real. We must assess what impact the propaganda will make on freedoms of thought, speech, and association, or the common good—to illustrate the harmful consequences and effects of the *anti*-democratic propaganda commonly used to:

1. Destroy individual security and liberty through the intimidation of individuals and groups.

36

2. Spread threats beyond any immediate victim of the propaganda.

3. Disparage and disrupt core institutions of government, neutering effective democratic governance.

4. Deny, delay, or distort policies, actions, and the rule of law, weakening truth, law, and justice.

5. Undermine a nation's military through delay or denial of funding, promotions, or other essentials for the effective operation of the military—to diminish national security.

6. Advance restrictive legislation and legal actions—to limit or remove voting rights and free association.

7. Facilitate the appointment and co-opting of autocratic persons to positions of oversight or influence for such key areas as voting, the courts, the military, education, the postal service, communication/media organizations, and decision-making institutions—to undermine the fairness, civility, and civic cohesion characteristic of democracy.

8. Enlarge controls on educational curricula and libraries—to limit free thought and inquiry.

9. Manipulate the Internet, social media platforms, and information networks through threats, hacks, hoaxes, fraud, or other harms—including "seeding" Google and other search engines with keywords and phrases to show up in "research," distorting "information discernment."[132]

10. Reshape everyday perceptions of us all, through "Big Lies," distorted facts, and memes that:

- Promise a mythical utopia, often fabricated from mythical past "glories."

- Accentuate the fears and desires of an autocrat's followers.

- Portray "others" as a shared enemy.

- Claim popular support through assertions like "a lot of people are saying."

- Bemoan "poor me and you" with followers, to galvanize unity.

Such "tells" reveal propaganda as more than chaotic word-salad. The apparently disjointed or sporadic outbursts and reactions of propagandists are designed to:

- Distract us from initiatives to strengthen democracy.
- Promote a self-image of the propagandist as a "strongman," thug, or mob-boss.
- Project the return to some mythical ideal past, which never arrives.

An alert population will identify these clues to how the propagandist shapes our attention, thought, and action. Any of us who values freedoms of thought, speech, religion, press, assembly, and petition against grievance caused by government, or the free choice of health services, job, travel, place of living, education, communication, or a host of freedoms frequently taken for granted should find ways to push back on the tough/sweet talk of propagandists who would deny our freedom.

Unfortunately, *anti*-democratic urgings appear in a variety of communications multiple times every day. Mostly, *breaking news* for example just seems to echo the propaganda of social media or media releases that promote a propagandist's interests and supposed significance. Showing the consequences and effects of the propagandist's claims on us as citizens is what matters.

A public who listens and speaks out is the root of democracy.[133]

6: ANTI-propaganda Action

...the sole true end of education is simply this: to teach [women and] men how to learn for themselves; and whatever instruction fails to do this is effort spent in vain.[134]

– Dorothy L. Sayers, 1947

The impact of thoughtful educators sometimes percolates into public awareness. News reports of the tragic shooting at Florida's Parkland High School in 2018 put a spotlight on the School's articulate students. Since that fateful day and now as graduates, they call for nationwide gun controls. Their impact in public service more broadly includes supporting the election of a fellow survivor of gun violence as the youngest representative in Congress. A better future grows from such efforts.

We all need to be more than bystanders in democracy. More judges, lawyers, and civic leaders are needed who will pre-empt the autocrat-propagandists gaming the law to corrupt the legal system. Likewise, we need more legislators, media anchors, pundits, journalists, media management, and others to break their habit of amplifying trite outrage by parroting propagandists' names, words, or memes.

Autocrat-propagandists rely on the failure to counter their propaganda to bathe us in distortions every day. Computerized and other

39

propagandists have just kept improving their microtargeting of us.[135] And foreign, state-sponsored incursions are virulent. When fully effective propaganda controls independent thought and action,[136] propagandists should be considered as menacing as military invaders.

Winning against propaganda requires a mind-set and actions akin to resistance efforts in authoritarian states.[137] Ramped-up efforts are needed to prosecute the wrongdoing of autocrat-propagandists and to expand popular support for democracy.[138] And each of us needs rules-of-thumb for useful action against those who invade our thought, speech, and actions—especially to help bolster the best antidote to propaganda, namely our own independent thinking.

Priority: Outwit Propagandists

To outwit propagandists, many insights found useful from countering or investigating propaganda and disinformation[139] can help address the varied goals of nations, organizations, or individuals.[140] A well-developed plan drawing on such insights will incorporate commitment to

Be First! Forewarning or prebunking propaganda appears to be most powerful. And psychological studies confirm the value of inoculation or *pre-exposing* audiences to a weak version of anticipated disinformation.[141] This is well-known to politicians who try to be first with good or bad news to pre-empt interpretations. Experimental studies of election campaigns are optimistic about such approaches to help deflect disinformation.[142]

Sustain concurrent initiatives against propaganda: "Put simply *...don't expect to counter the firehose of falsehood with the squirt gun of truth.*"[143]

Engage multiple, credible spokespersons and communication channels to debunk propaganda that's already in play.[144] Repeating the propagandist's words is almost always a bad idea. Studies suggest that effective debunking of mis/disinformation is difficult—the more so when it's already been much repeated or little-challenged.

40

Highlight briefly and tangibly in lively, resonant ways what are the most harmful effects of a propagandist's deeds,[145] claims, or urgings. Illustrate the effects on us. Do "not worry so much about countering propaganda that contributes to effects that are not of concern."[146]

Be Ready to rapidly push back on potentially damaging rumors, polemic, and lies. The tabloid-based autocrat undermines the mass media and avoids interviews or cross-questioning, yet many members of the mass media remain megaphones for this scurrilous nonsense. Especially during political campaigns, it's vital to be equipped to quickly answer, consciously ignore, or dampen inflammatory claims.

Push for law reform and longer-term fixes. While the priority is to preempt and dismantle the harm of day-to-day propaganda, longer-term fixes must also be addressed. "Ideas for reducing the flood of disinformation abound," including regulation or self-regulation of "the supply or demand side."[147] Even though energies and attention are stretched, we must decide what relatively few longer-term fixes warrant support.

Detecting Propaganda

How propaganda works remains difficult for many people to fathom. A first step for deflecting propaganda or disinformation is to project the harm likely to follow from a propagandist's claims or urgings. Although propaganda is the art of the simple, its processes, effects, successes, or failures can be hard to objectively describe or measure. Jacques Ellul's book *Propaganda* offers the most comprehensive understanding of the social and psychological principles at work; with Garth Jowett and Victoria O'Donnell's *Propaganda and Persuasion* providing a much-valued introduction.[148]

Propaganda is a dynamic of a mass group experiencing a *firehose of information*. Its effectiveness depends on at least some members of the group interacting with each other, within as well as across sub-groups, to influence the dynamic of the mass group. Ellul cautions about experiments with "a particular method of propaganda on small groups

41

and in small doses—at which moment it ceases to be propaganda."[149] Much needed are further actionable insights concluded from investigating propaganda "in the wild," with reality as the laboratory.

As noted earlier, propaganda like any communication is heard differently by different people. We acknowledge this about communication for our one-on-one conversations by intuitively using differently nuanced approaches to engage with different people. Words, images, or symbols are "neither fixed nor unified... [in their meaning, and] ...audiences [do not]...consist merely of like-minded segments,"[150] despite what pollsters or other audience analysts may assert or imply. Appreciating how propaganda really works as it lands differently with different audience members is essential to address what's going on.

For example, even when a crowd chants back at a propagandist some slogan or incantation, the communication takes shape individually in the minds of each member of the crowd. People united in action to deliver the propagandist's desired action do so from a variety of interpretations driving people to action. Understanding this is needed to engage members of the crowd in the dialogue that destroys propaganda.

It's important to appreciate that propagandists employ many tools and methods, since "strategies that may be effective at countering or neutralizing one type of misinformation may not work against others."[151] Propaganda uses many different types and degrees of truth and truth out of context.[152] A *party line* or a propagandist's style may be drummed out within a background of quite credible information, including selected facts or *alternative facts*.[153]

Soundly informed skepticism can deal with many of the propagandist's part-truths, distortions, lies, insults, threats, unjust accusations, character assassinations, or promises of utopia. But anyone looking only for blatant lies or preoccupied with a propagandist's supposed intentions can become diverted by *red herrings*—and too readily fall prey to a well-developed propaganda campaign.[154]

Recognizing Devices

Awareness of rhetorical methods and devices can help with understanding propaganda as more than "tall stories,"[155] or isolated statements, or only what adversarial governments do. From classical through recent times, teachers of rhetoric, philosophy, and related fields have offered ways to analyze a wide range of propaganda devices and common fallacies that propagandists use.

Eleanor MacLean and Randal Marlin outline a robust list of fallacies and some lesser-known propaganda devices used to manipulate an audience. MacLean describes deceptive practices involving language, *Bold assertions, Selective omission, Quoting out of context, Twisting and distortion, Meshing fact with opinion,* and others.[156] Marlin outlines logical fallacies, including *Ad hominem argument, False cause, Hasty generalization, Ignoring the question, Ignoring the logical force and direction of an argument, Begging the question, False analogy, Amphiboly* (sentence constructions that can be parsed differently to get different meanings), and *Accident* (treating the nonessential as essential).[157]

From 1937-1942, Clyde R. Miller spearheaded a notable effort specifically against propaganda through the Institute for Propaganda Analysis (IPA) in New York. This initiative sought to limit the impact of propaganda on democracy by bolstering the public's ability to think critically, for well-considered discussion of daily events. In 1939, Miller said:

> There are three ways to deal with propaganda - first, to suppress it; second, to try to answer it by counter propaganda; third, to analyze it.[158]

The IPA was established with the support of the retailer Edward A. Filene and academic Kirtley Mather. As Michael Sproule observes, this Institute fused "academic and practical progressivism into an organized antipropaganda critique."[159] Critics of the IPA failed "to distinguish between healthy skepticism and dysfunctional cynicism."[160] Perhaps most contributing to the suspension of the IPA's operations were changing viewpoints among some of its leaders when the United States entered World War II, as well as the difficulty of continuing to raise operating funds in the "changed social climate."[161]

The IPA disseminated seven devices that propagandists use to tap prejudice and other emotions, as well as "ABCs" to help people highlight or suppress their own judgment. Description and examples of the IPA's seven devices, *Name-calling, Glittering generality, Transfer, Testimonial, Plain folks, Card stacking, and Bandwagon,* along with the ABCs, remain readily available and widely used.[162] They have helped many people understand and deal at a basic level with propaganda.

Inarguably, these are just some of the ways to help detect propaganda. The easier propagandists to call out are those who say the outright opposite of what they do. More challenging are conjurers of euphemism[163] or maestros of the mealy-mouthed—especially any enabled by focus groups to parse and tailor what "best words" to direct at us, like *prosperity, results, renewal, security,* or a litany of words that are promoted into conversation without any matching actions that are required to deliver solutions for people. Instead of parroting a propagandist's vacuous words, it's best to amplify what actions are needed for real solutions.

Of course, it's important to try to spot lies. To help with this, law enforcement and counterespionage interviewers explain indicators like *Failing to answer, Non-specific denial, Reluctance or refusal to answer, Answering a question with a question,* or *Requesting a question be repeated.*[164] These are considered significant when two or more occur. Despite ongoing research though, methods for spotting lies are not necessarily assured.[165]

For dealing with the ever-increasing waves of digital lies, librarians and others have also developed helpful ways to verify the accuracy of claims, including checking the changes made on Internet web pages, using the Wayback Machine or other methods.[166] Researchers using large language models continue to increase the accuracy of digital tools to enable large-scale detection of "fake news" and misinformation.[167]

Ongoing Education

An urgent priority is to massively expand education enhancing the ability of adults, youth, and children to assess public discourse—to discern, analyze, and synthesize reality. Unfortunately, during recent centuries, as both education and the vote became more generally available in Western democracies, too many education curricula jettisoned valuable tools to differentiate sense from nonsense in public discourse.[168] People educated from the mid- to later twentieth century onwards have often had to rely on self-education for logic or smatterings of dialectics and rhetorical skills.

A sorry decline in rhetorical education throughout the United States is outlined in David Fleming's essay, "Fear of Persuasion in the English Language Arts." He observes:

> ...if we identify persuasion with manipulation and pandering only, we fail to recognize a realm of influence-seeking that is neither of those, that tries to move others while still respecting their autonomy...[169]

From the mid-twentieth century, many educators developed "other frameworks...to teach critical thinking... [that mostly] avoided directly confronting society's leading persuaders and intractable problems... [and] ...emphasized the internal psychology of the thinker."[170] A range of programs need strengthening to educate thoughtful and articulate citizens.[171]

There is "significant evidence that media literacy training can help people identify false stories and unreliable news sources," empowering "motivated individuals to take control of their media" use. As a whole-of-nation strategy to counter propaganda, media literacy "suffers challenges in speed, scale, and targeting."[172] Even so, some nations are investing substantially in practical education of children, youths, and adults—including diplomats, members of defense forces, and other groups.[173] Renee Hobbs and Sandra McGee provide perspective on these programs, many of which have developed novel delivery modes and other innovations for learning that increase understandings of propaganda.[174]

Beyond the many efforts to educate future generations through media literacy,[175] nationwide initiatives in the United States are also strengthening civics education. In addition to the children and youth for whom programs like the relatively recent "Educating for American Democracy"[176] are designed, such programs could be valuable for many

45

adults. College programs in civics, literacy, rhetoric, writing, media, or other fields also provide models to encourage collaborative inquiry into community problems. These programs develop democratic deliberation, re-structuring dialogues to encourage personal and public change through building "community literacy" in students[177]–advancing both educational goals and improved community understandings.

Research Insights

During the last seven years or so, the explosion of research into disinformation, conspiracy theories, fake news, and related areas is developing concepts of misinformation broadly defined, digital detection tools, or psychological understandings, particularly in relation to social media and mass media. A continuing challenge with this research is inconsistency defining core terms and concepts. The many thousands of research investigations that are concluded or underway require ongoing curation to distill what might be usefully put to work at scale.[178]

Some earlier studies suggest the value of assuring multi-faceted, pro-active initiatives to counter propaganda. Recommendations include

- mounting media literacy education to reduce "the persuasive efficacy" of propaganda,
- driving a wedge among adversaries,
- inoculating with information to reduce an "audience's potential to be influenced,"
- debunking to replace "incorrect information," and
- developing new regulations and other "strategies to counter propagandists and disinformation."[179]

Important studies include "Propaganda of the Deed and Its Anarchist Origins," "Countering Hamas and Hezbollah Propaganda," "Defending against Russian Propaganda," "IS's Strategic Communication Tactics," and "The Evolution of Terrorist Propaganda in Cyberspace."[180]

More recent research examines networks and the effectiveness of interventions,[181] which include prebunking, boosting (psychological inoculation, critical thinking, and media/information literacy), nudging (accuracy primes and social norm nudges), debunking (fact-checking), and automatic labeling.[182] Still other insights are available concerning the content, motivations, and processes of conspiracy theorists, along with learning from ex-believers about individual journeys in and out of conspiracy theories online.[183]

Propaganda is described in some research as realizing "ideological goals through intentional distortions." This work seeks to highlight: (1) the role of "true" information; (2) the influence of context; (3) the importance of repetition, not only as a rhetorical device but related to the means of distribution and dissemination; and (4) the part played by audiences themselves in the cyclical flows of digital information.[184] Other studies show how the preoccupation that many people have with social media facilitates their ready participation as audience members to amplify propaganda.[185]

The editors of *The Sage Handbook of Propaganda* call for studies of the "effects of propaganda, particularly on democratic and authoritarian systems and on public opinion, over time."[186] And propagandists exploit both positive and negative features of a society's culture. This makes at least as important studies to secure better understanding of how these features of culture predispose us to accept propaganda.

Whether for nations, organizations, or individuals, deciding priorities to outwit propagandists requires a developed understanding of the continuously evolving propaganda networks and processes. The ability to deal productively with controversy and conflicts of opinion has characterized the advancement of social and scientific progress from the seventeenth and eighteenth centuries.[187] As we go forward, ever-better critical abilities, conversation skills, and system resources are essential to deal effectively with the outrageous claims, polemic, scandal, or other distortions of truth by propagandists.

7: Deflection and Deterrence

No newis is bettir than evill newis.[188]

– King James I, 1616

A politician who uses "strategies to achieve collaborative power" within a democratic system is very different to one who uses "strategies to grab coercive power for relatively naked or revolutionary political action."[189] The latter will ordinarily use propaganda to exploit narcissistic needs of both the propagandist and followers, who "consider themselves superior" to others.[190]

It's commonly observed that this propagandist amplifies fears about *others,* along with claims that these *others* cause harm to *collective wellbeing.*[191] It's widely thought that a propagandist gathers followers among those who feel neglected and aggrieved by politicians or so-called elites. If so, what can we do to deal with fears in a propagandist's followers? If we look to theories of fear for guidance, we find that previous applications of fear theory to engage the public's support to counter terror activity or security threats had limited success. These theories were "largely developed through experimentation rather than in the field."[192]

And beyond fears, the wide-ranging motivations for aligning with propagandists include seeking fun,[193] attention, recognition, and belonging, or satisfying curiosity, greed, or graft. But what's certain is that, as with a viral pandemic, a virulent propagandist doesn't "just disappear."

Debriefing ex-believers who journey in and out of conspiracy theories may offer useful clues to deal with the tribe-like devotion of a propagandist's followers.[194] What appears effective to reengage the propagandist's most polarized followers back with the real world is painstakingly systematic involvement through one-on-one or one-on-two discussions.[195]

Ongoing are explorations to engage citizens in local decision-making in ways that strengthen democracy, including consideration of the potential applicability of the Swiss Cantonal Parliament model.[196] Other approaches designed around the principles of college programs that for decades have built "community literacy" in students may prove helpful.[197] A common thread is building cooperative efforts that tangibly benefit the community in which participants live. In contrast, the pseudo-democratic authoritarian is all about fabricating a parallel fantasy-reality.

Fighting Fabrication

Understanding and dealing with propaganda requires truth-seeking and "quality problem-solving conversations."[198] For dialogue that bolsters democracy, it's necessary to step outside established zones of comfort within institutions, professions, job descriptions, or allied socializations. Some activists, educators, journalists, judges, members of the media, or others do manage to begin the simple dialogue that causes propaganda to cease. By reasserting "political rationality," these individuals do much "to build, maintain and strengthen liberal democracy."[199]

They help deflect aspiring autocrats. Countering these propagandists' rude, contrarian antics is vital to deny the consolidation of power through the incitement of otherwise little-checked harms. Unimpeded, propagandists continuously undermine the rule of law and effective government. This accelerates democratic backsliding, most defined as:

...deterioration of at least one of three pillars of democracy: free and fair elections, protection of broad political rights and personal freedoms, as well as the rule of law...[200]

That propaganda is commonly a tool of presumed powerful political, commercial, religious, or military figures is disincentive to prosecution or legislation addressing the harms caused by these bad actors. Prosecutions of influential bad actors are much less than required–not least because of the limited resources of public prosecutors' offices.

Yet some prosecutors and judges, and even some legislators, manage to function beyond buggy-pace in a nanosecond world. Apparently unhampered by self-preserving caution or other presumptions so common in their professions, these individuals step beyond platitudes like *The wheels of justice grind slowly, but exceedingly fine,* to advance the contrary maxim *Justice delayed is justice denied.*

Deterring Harm

These prosecutors and judges interpret *imminent* at something approaching the speed reality requires. Yet they seem only able to very slowly bring some perpetrators to account for more egregious harms, like defamation, fraud, or perjury. When gaming the rule of law is the rule of play, remedy is needed at a speed to meet the need.

Policymakers who can find any bipartisan alignment must likewise address the ever-present flood of harmful disinformation. Glimmers of hope mainly appear in the European Union, which systematically executes support and direction for stakeholders seeking to mitigate the impact of disinformation.[201] Policymakers and civic leaders must still be pushed well beyond their limited efforts to date to counter even obviously false information causing harm. For example, the action of United States attorneys-general against Internet platforms should have occurred long ago to address harms to children. And it's reasonable to push for state and federal action in similar ways to protect adults from harmful effects of social media.

Required Reassessment

The proliferation of propaganda to incite insurrection or violence that harms democracy itself and our fellow citizens requires that we reassess the effectiveness of legal protections.

Especially serious is that fully functioning propaganda controls the thought and actions of large population groups. Curiously, a clichéd story in the legal profession proffers that shouting *Fire!* in a crowded movie theater is not acceptable, yet propaganda immediately threatening democracy largely is?

With bravado or defiance, autocrat-propagandists in the United States often falsely claim their speech is protected under The First Amendment— which does not apply for speech advancing particular illegal activity. This includes lies that:

> unambiguously have no or little social value...and also cause cognizable harms (as well as sometimes yielding undeserved benefits for the liar)... [which includes] ...fraud, perjury, ...and making false statements to public officials.[202]

It's well past time for more action than scholars or pundits rightly pointing this out.

Civic leaders must take the lead on actionable offenses, instead of dodging their responsibility to do so, sometimes by repeating incorrect platitudes about free speech. This just further empowers a propagandist's undermining of the rule of law. Likewise, pursuit of criminal or civil penalties on propagandists must be stepped up for violating public trust through perjury, tax evasion, espionage, and mail or wire fraud during fundraising or merchandise sales.

Citizens theoretically can seek remedy for propagandists' criminal or civil wrongs, like defamation or fraud. But an individual mounting legal action against a propagandist incurs substantial financial and emotional burdens, on top of dealing with the ever-increasing threats of physical harm from a propagandist's followers.

Action Against Lies

Unsurprisingly, scholars concerned about the adequacy of the civil tort system to provide redress for the harms caused by lies conclude that:

> the criminal law delivers real sanctions; ...shame and stigma accompanying criminal punishment [is]...not dependent on a willing victim to pursue punishment...[and] ...a consequentialist approach that employs Feinberg's reasoning not only justifies, but demands the criminalization of certain egregious forms of lying.[203]

Following close examination of the main categories of lies, two scholars propose a new crime focused solely on the lies that harm another person or entity. Their sample clause for the new crime considers "that lies should only be criminalized if they are intended to cause serious harm and if said harm results,"[204] namely:

> A person is guilty of egregious lying causing serious harm when...[she or] he knowingly lies to another person (1) with the intent to cause serious harm to that person; and (2) serious harm occurs as a result of the lie. As used in this section, a "lie" means a false statement made to another person in oral or written form.[205]

With ever-proliferating harms from disinformation, the pressure should and likely will mount on civic leaders to do something about the ongoing exploitation of snails-paced legal procedures, as well as to close the substantive and procedural loopholes in the law that propagandists exploit. Not even codification, however, may remedy the fictions surrounding "puffery," which judicial interpretations in commercial settings concurrently consider a "vague statement"[206] and "assumed not to work,"[207] yet, paradoxically, supposedly helps citizens by offering assurances to fulfill expectations.[208]

Changes to law, such as the provision in France that enabled "judges to order the removal of false information during electoral periods"[209] will spotlight tensions in the continuum between censorship and free speech principles in practice.

What's Acceptable?

What's very clear is that neglecting to promptly hold autocrat-propagandists to account is unacceptably harmful. And unlike the infamous juggernaut autocrat-propagandists try to resemble, propagandists do have some weaknesses in common. Some of these may prove useful to deter behavior, beyond the financial penalties imposed through successful prosecutions. For example, the combination of narcissism and greed that drives torrents of "what-about-me-ism" in an autocrat is an Achilles heel.

Firstly, there's the opportunity to increase media coverage of anyone other than the propagandist. An opportunity with similar effect is to further amplify the propagandist's declines in fundraising, without the usual, habitual use of photographs, video, or quotes of the propagandist.

Secondly, serious scrutiny of the dark effects of an autocrat's alleged criminality on the rest of us may help. Even though an autocrat-propagandist may commonly use corrupt practices for self-advancement, some veneer of legality is required until absolute power is secured.

It's not yet routine in modern Western democracies to ostracize corrupt autocrats. Many who support insurrection remain effectively immune, even from prosecution. Interestingly, ostracism originated as a process to protect democracy from threat in ancient Athens. Each year the assembly of citizens decided whether to hold an ostracism or not.[210] The process:

> ...first emerged to protect the system, from those who intend to abolish democracy...[and]...can be considered an expression of the people's belief in democracy and their desire to protect their government.[211]

There was no need to prove the accusation or claim causing the exile of ostracism. The vote of citizens required an offender to leave Athens for ten years. This was also practice in some other Greek city-states.[212]

As naysayers attempt to downplay the impacts that propaganda and disinformation make on us all, now is the time to get ahead of propagandists.

8: Going Forward

The only way to find a solution is to act.[213]

– Maria Ressa, 2022

Anyone who still believes the children's rhyme that closes with *words will never hurt me*[214] is either not paying attention, or more concerning, does not want to. Propaganda impacts what everyone thinks or does. In both autocratic and democratic states, people must deal with propaganda in endlessly engulfing waves. Inaction or inappropriate reactions to its impact empowers an autocrat. Autocrats and aspiring autocrats rely greatly on a population's self-censorship to manage dissent.[215]

Nicholas O'Shaughnessy has illuminated the strategy autocrats employ to develop pseudo-democracy. By using "the magnifying glass of TV and the Internet,"[216] they sow confusion, make pseudo-reality plausible, manage symbolism and perceptions of history, myth, or existential threat, then follow up with soft power in an evangelistic mode and with physical coercion. The objective is to secure acquiescence, not belief, to create "conformists." To secure and retain power, the autocrat propagandist "offers a worldview that is simple, coherent, and easily communicated ...founded on some idea of a nationalist utopia."[217]

Resistance and Resilience

Fortunately, a propagandist's threat to freedoms also has an unintended consequence of fueling resistance and resilience in people who are allergic to such control. While lip-service to democracy may satisfy a propagandist's followers, democracy nurtures in many others a "fluid and many-sided" personality[218] with intuition and commitment for what it takes to expand "rights and liberties to everybody."[219] A wide range of such civic virtues nurture personal and group resilience and understandings of personal liberty, mutual respect, and tolerance as lived experiences–tangibly impacting citizenship, civil action, education, and other personal or social understandings and initiatives that protect and promote the autonomy of citizens.[220]

Common approaches used to resist propagandists are "speaking out, to humor, to avoiding confrontation, [which]...may not work as 'constructive resistances.'"[221] Much detection and dealing with propaganda focuses on revealing faulty reasoning, lies and part-truths, or appeals to audience emotions, to discredit the supposed intentions of a propagandist. But as long ago as 2018 in the United States at least, it was publicly acknowledged that multiple, dispersed warnings about intent, propaganda mechanisms, or various fact-checking approaches[222] via however intelligent and penetrating commentary, blistering advertisements, mockery, hype, or even legal probes are no match for an ongoing onslaught of unfettered propaganda.[223]

It's surely important to ferret out "the tactics and hidden interests of persuasive campaigns,"[224] but to motivate action it's necessary to visualize what's significant to people's lives–focusing on just a relatively few, digestible concerns to stimulate action and encourage new habits.[225] For motivation against propaganda to be useful, communication efforts must occur at a scale that energizes meaningfully large population groups to actively resist autocrats.[226]

Differently nuanced methods are required to tackle different types of propaganda, or different phases in a propagandist's efforts, especially in different cultures. For example, although "political rhetoric in Scandinavia is generally less hostile and polarised than in many other European countries – and especially the US – the last 20 years have shown right-wing movements using increasingly hostile and aggressive rhetoric."[227] Perceptions and expectations concerning power, individualism, competition, security, norms, or restraint vary greatly among cultural groups,[228] within and beyond national boundaries. Certainly though, much more than emotion-charged inaction is needed to deal with insurgency,[229] including when dealing with terrorists against democracy.

Get Ready

As mentioned earlier, some researchers suggest prebunking as a particularly effective approach to blunt misinformation.[230] This requires anticipating a propagandist's disruptive actions and hubris. Both immediately and longer term, a priority must be to continuously monitor, detect, and draw attention to the specific harms inherent in the claims or presumptions of propaganda.

Mostly, a propagandist's contrarian behaviors become very predictable. Slogans or specific wordings and actions are commonly recycled in copy-cat from other places or earlier times. For example, among the many occasions that a propagandist's "reality" imitates fiction or vice-versa is a representation of events in 1946 within an episode of the British television series, *Foyle's War,* first broadcast in 2015. A propagandist's public speech is scripted with the eerily familiar catchwords of today's propagandists, including "stuck in hell holes," "illegal aliens," "stolen jobs," "take back our streets," and "Make Britain great again."[231]

With a bit of creativity, it's quite straightforward to anticipate many claims or actions of a propagandist and then to brainstorm effective strategies, to be ready for strategic response. Compiling an "issues file" of draft media releases or pre-drafted outlines for news stories or other materials ahead of time provides a good resource for pre-emptively blocking or quickly deflecting most claims and antics. These materials may be especially effective when developed to address *anti*-democracy insurgencies, like the ten areas listed at the conclusion of the earlier chapter on "Counter *Anti*-democracy."

Undercutting a propagandist's presumptions, claims, and actions is done simply enough by drawing attention to how these will impact the lives of family, friends, neighbors, or workmates. Individually and collectively, we should progressively expect and request similar forethought more often from aspiring and elected legislators, the media, judiciary, tech platform executives, and any other individuals or groups engaged in the public sphere.

Stand Up

What most empowers a propagandist are reactions. Instead of reactively taking to social media, or devising that media exposé of this or that propagandist, or feeling threatened, or otherwise responding to impulses for fight or flight when our raw nerves are touched off by a propagandist's emotive nonsense, it's surely time to take a pause. And much more is needed than switching off media and tech devices, although at least occasionally this could help gain some perspective. Push back requires concerted effort that motivates additional purposeful efforts.

Our preference for what's "free and easy" prioritizes daily living. And putting time and effort into critically assessing public assertions, proposals, policies, events, and actions can be challenging. Ever-increasing amounts of data, along with propaganda designed to discredit its reliability, prevent people from making judgments and forming opinions.[232]

Also working against thoughtfulness and analytical approaches are human capacities for self-delusion.[233] People most interested in a matter are prone to mistakenly believe themselves best able to discriminate the falsity of claims. Ironically, the more vigorously that we scrutinize propagandist drivel, the more likely we'll accept at least some propaganda, since it's often based on plausible presumptions. High repetition and frequent exposure enhance how plausibly even an outrageous lie is perceived.

Individually and as a society, it's especially important to stand up to the now too common, virulent propaganda that abuses or threatens people's personality or safety. It's hard to figure why such behavior is tolerated and not called out more at community gatherings, such as school board meetings, or legislatures, or the supermarket checkout! Propaganda directed against people in this way constitutes abuse and monopolizes the mind.[234] Another insidious effect is to stifle the dialogue, debate, and participation essential to democracy.

Such verbal abuse is no longer tolerated elsewhere in the community, like the home or workplace. But perhaps due to a mix of being taken by surprise, trying to be polite, or avoiding confrontation, or the financial and emotional demands of tackling the more egregious of these events legally, the propagandist in the public arena rolls on, somewhat like a juggernaut, too long immune.

Ways to remedy related inadequacies in the law need to be made "imminent," as most of us outside the legal profession define the word. At the time of occurrence of some abuse, individuals or chairpersons of meetings or groups are increasingly objecting to and moderating that behavior. This ordinarily requires some verbal, Whac-A-Mole skills. Mastery of the quick come-back and the ability to partner polemic with humor can be valuable to advance serious matters.

Media Change

The tabloid-based, sensational outrage and antics of a propagandist deliver a daily spigot of potential "news." For decades, media presenters, journalists, and media management have navigated restrictive aspects of company policy, diminishing budgets, limited time, talent migration, and other limits on efforts to sustain audiences. Unsurprisingly, the hyperbole, and even milder exaggeration of autocrat-propagandists, combined with provocative ambiguity, seem to fulfill a headline-writer's dream for attracting audience attention, whether connected to reality or not. No one has all the answers for dealing with this *de facto* power of a propagandist over the media.

But some members of the media are exploring ways to lessen the impact of propaganda, such as through paraphrase, or otherwise truly editing a propagandist's drivel. It should be fine for moderators on broadcast media or editors in the print media to use different words than the propagandist's bad words, distorted truth (and lies) again, and again, and again—and to challenge it as propaganda. After all, this is little different than the responsibility to prevent dissemination of libel and slander—and unchecked, propaganda is at least as harmful.

And ever since the televised presidential debates in the United States in 1960, we've known that pundits who soon afterwards comment on what public figures say have more power than the original remarks. A variation for dealing with a propagandist that one thoughtful television anchor developed is to present a propagandist's comments split screen, alongside the anchor's reactions. This is just one approach to handle a propagandist's avoidance of interviews or cross-questioning, to cynically use the media as a megaphone.

News managers could take up more of the many suggestions long available to address such concerns. At the very least, directly and regularly "ask the public [...including former followers...] what they think of your news coverage—and listen to what they say."[235] Media audiences do expect journalism to be more solutions based[236] and less obsessed with news as conflict, celebrity, disaster, sex, crime, or violence.[237] It would be helpful, for example, to roll back *breaking news* so that it is only what is truly urgent or directly impacts most of us.[238]

Likewise, some diligence calling out false dichotomy would be a good move. Mostly unchallenged in the media is one of the propagandist's oldest rhetorical tricks of claiming to protect a freedom by leaving decision on a matter to "free decision" as a "local or state option." As far back as 1854, Abraham Lincoln showed how to powerfully deflect this trick, by calling out the inhumanity of making good people choose between self-interest and what is moral.[239] But this propagandist's rhetorical trick is still given unmoderated airplay on many so-called states-rights issues. It deserves to be called out as advocacy of self-interest, as Lincoln did.

Serious efforts more widely are needed in the media to "bring back into the fold those who have shunned the news for the intolerably trivial circus it has become."[240] Ongoing handwringing in the media and in journalism education circles to "regain" audiences requires better innovation based on truly listening to audiences, many of whom share fears of what happens to media freedom in autocracies. Immediate actions to meet immediate needs are required of the media and each of us.

Community Engagement

How else might you bring value and encourage young, savvy individuals who have the chops to execute needed change? If you're a joiner, join and recruit others to join an action group that puts pressure and expects results from civic officials on matters you care about. Whether by interrogating, cooperating with, or operating alongside the efforts of civic leaders, the judiciary, activists, and the media, it is open to each of us to stand up to a propagandist's polemic by joining or commencing efforts that make a difference.

Perhaps unsurprisingly, even in nations where volunteerism is strong, the participation in political organizations or causes tends to be just a small fraction of other volunteering.[241] A few strong and organized voices can make a real difference relatively quickly to the tenor and direction of politics, especially locally and regionally. Each of us must find ways to participate. Failure to do so enables *pseudo-populists* to infiltrate the selection of candidates for political office who are less than suitable.

Whether within a political organization or separately, it can also be effective to invite four to six other "doers" to come together face-to-face or online, say weekly or as you can, for brainstorming about ways to help advance real community needs. After inviting aspiring or elected representatives, regulators, and administrators to brief your group on their plans, proposals, or ideas, your follow-on actions can include

60

interrogating, monitoring, or supporting some suggestions or initiatives. Or you may commit support to personal advocacy.

Citizens, members of the media, civic officials, or whistleblowers who develop clear aims in pursuing an overall plan can help defeat political subversion.[242] In a democracy, beyond voting and working to help ensure that effective, democratic leaders are elected, individuals can help make democracy thrive in other ways. Just by writing a letter (not a tweet or email) to your elected representative requesting action on something you care about denies the acquiescence that the autocrat seeks. Ask for and expect a reply, and follow up if you do not get one, until you do get a satisfactory (not a mealy-mouthed) reply.

For push back against autocrats in autocratic states, developing democracies, or established democracies that are resisting back-sliding, well-planned, strategic use of social media may allow people to share information, grow group cohesion, resist dominance, and fight for freedom. Maria Ressa's inspiring efforts to stand up to a dictator in the Philippines is one example. She focuses four layers of action to "help shorten the time it takes to correct the lies…[and] …have civil society act… [with] …three goals: scale, impact and deterrence."[243]

In both democratic and autocratic states, analogous efforts with goals suited to local conditions can focus an activist group's efforts to mesh with appropriate coalitions, such as "civil society groups, business organizations, and religious groups." Follow-on efforts then link with university and other educational efforts, and engage other key professionals, like lawyers and journalists.[244]

Unaddressed, propaganda redefines what's considered important, diverting attention from policy and governance that matters. Effectively countering the propaganda that seeks pseudo-democracy requires each of us to decide how to take action.

What more can you do? What will you do?

APPENDIX - It's Time for Plain Talk - Pundit Propaganda - It's the Propaganda STU*** - Rip Van Who? - What to Do[245]

It's Time for Plain Talk

Augustus Saint-Gaudens, an American sculptor of the Beaux-Arts generation, once remarked that "...it's the way a thing's done that makes it right or wrong."[246]

When it comes to public talk, I believe we're long overdue for some plain talk about what we should accept as right. Too many public conversations now (obviously, tweets too) are just, well, unacceptable, wrong, off, or cringeworthy. Take your pick, or waste energy on expletives and likely you'll be closest to right.

Here, I'm not referring to comments like someone who described an opponent as "*simply a shiver looking for a spine to run up.*"[247] With variants tracing back to at least 1966, the endurance of this artful and possibly apt gibe might be welcome for many to hear (except the latest target).

Doublethink

No, what we need plain talk about is what George Orwell's description of Newspeak helped spotlight, namely "doublethink," "doubletalk," and that close relative "doublespeak."

This is:

> ...a process of indoctrination whereby the subject is expected to accept as true that which is clearly false, or to simultaneously accept two mutually contradictory beliefs as correct, often in contravention to one's own memories or sense of reality. (Wikipedia)

Why then are there not more of us carrying out Orwell's urging to jeer "...loudly enough, [to] send some worn out and useless phrase– some...lump of verbal refuse...into the dustbin where it belongs."[248]

Fact-checks

For example, there are good reasons to believe that fact-checking, as it's mostly done, is a fool's fantasy. Firstly, once prejudices are established

63

and continuously reinforced, including through the mail, media, or social media, the "tribe" will not believe criticism from any source about a tribal leader's corruption or malfeasance.

Secondly, very clear is that so-called fact-checking, or otherwise restating a message by repeating it (even in the negative), just reinforces the original propaganda. Both the believers and the undecided will focus on the original false message and ignore that little word "NOT" or other negation that the fact checker inserts. The negative is as invisible as the cyclists whom car drivers genuinely don't see on the road.

To Counter

There are right ways to counter the emergence of the ideological offspring of Joseph Goebbels and Leni Riefenstahl. These include:

1. Ignore any verbal refuse designed to distract, deny, or delay—by all means, counter with the truth but, please, oh please, stop repeating the words of the original—you're just being a megaphone for what you oppose.

2. Listen up, friends in the media, there's not much that a bad actor fears more than being ignored—at the very least, please: **stop** using or repeating a bad actor's name; **stop** repeating direct quotes in the lower thirds of the television screen; and, **stop** showing "B-Roll" or photos of a bad actor, instead of doing your job to paraphrase any comments, if needed at all.

3. Encourage leaks of sensitive information that expose lies and fraud.

4. Reverse any serious lie right back onto the liar—use words more like the graffiti artist who sprays a mustache, beard, or horns onto a propaganda poster.

5. Exponentially grow networks of person-to-person communications, especially through personal emails, and personalized tweets.

Finally, if you believe you can win doing it right, and you put in the effort to communicate vigorously and well, you will win.

| *June 25, 2020*

Pundit Propaganda

Propagandist Pundits play too much with our perception. Will such folks ever appreciate that if we really do hanker for the current equivalent of *performing geese, roosters, & a musical donkey,* we'll find a real circus.

NOT talking here about the so obvious pundits whom we regrettably notice too much–these are the self-servers, who routinely speak conspiracy lies, or so much that's outrageous, that, if they had a moral compass, or any of the faith that some of them claim, their comments would surely head them hellward. NOR those mentioned recently in an opinion article in the newspaper, which suggested that pundits should own up when they get something wrong, just like the rest of us do, when inevitably in life we make a mistake.

Important as those are to address, more important are pundits who try to put truthful perspective yet fail. And these pundits are important because of their potential! These are the folks who too often fail by being unwitting propagandists, constantly parroting the words and claims of some grifter, charlatan, propagandist, or other pretender–thereby publicizing the pretender's original claims. Particularly dangerous and destructive to democracy now are these prevalent and persistent pundits.

Ever since the first televised presidential debates in the United States in 1960, we've known that pundits who soon afterwards comment on what public figures say have more power than the original remarks. As mentioned in an earlier blog post, this was already apparent as long ago as 1943, when the brilliant pundit Martin Esslin–well before he famously described the theater of the absurd–participated in counter-propaganda radio broadcasts. His role was to immediately analyze Hitler's speeches, and Esslin's analyses–which were unfavorable to the Nazis–were broadcast in German into occupied countries, where people were allowed to listen only to radio broadcasts in German.

Today, we need more pundits who use their own words more, to comment truthfully, positively, and plainly. To do this, many need to stop repeating the language of pretenders. For example, when will people's attraction to alliteration give way to common sense? Should be plain as day that, if you keep quoting the audience-tested, much propagated slogan "St** the St***," you're helping the propagandist by spreading bad words (and lies) again, and again, and again, etc.

And it should be just fine for moderators on broadcast media or editors in the print media to use different words to challenge this as propaganda. No different than the responsibility to prevent dissemination of libel and slander, and unchecked propaganda is at least as dangerous.

Dear Pundit, if you really must have a slogan to repeat, or a bumper sticker to put up somewhere prominently, how about the alliterative **"Stop the Stupid."** Or, instead of still repeating "no fr**d was found," just dump the negatives—and say what's **Fair** for **Freedom** of thought, speech, and association. It's simple to do when you remember what's at stake.

But apparently these pundits feel purified by putting a negative in front of their free publicity for some pretender—whom they ironically often decry—then do detailed forensics, reusing the pretender's fantasy verbiage, and repeat the original words and claims endlessly, sometimes putting "not" in front; mistakenly believing that "not" has some power that it actually lacks.

For example, if I said to you "Don't WALK on the grass," likely you'd hear most prominently the verb "walk" and what follows it, even if I'd not capitalized=shouted this verb, or if I'd used "not" instead of the barely noticeable contraction ...*n't!* Have you noticed also that verbs are more powerful in getting our attention than nouns and negatives... or just about any other bit of language? Since this imperative or instruction form of the verb is especially powerful and attention-getting because it rarely occurs in conversation, there's added inclination for your brain to totally ignore the negative and hear something more like "Go ahead, you (or y'all) go walk on the grass!!"

Out of habit, or dancing around legalisms, or ignorance, or just being lazy though, people do negate or double-negate comments, all the time.

Some even double-negate themselves into insulting followers, as was reported recently.

It really is simple to rephrase or paraphrase, to purify the puerile and pernicious. How about just saying "X & Y have occurred, and Z suggests/ed this remedy..." instead of the usual pattern, "This killer fog that I'm showing you again and again will not go away anytime soon." Maybe cross the street, so-to-speak, to find someone who will offer a remedy to pursue, rather than continuing to provide a platform for some "Desdemona-downer" pretender! Or, for additional thoughts on what language to use, please re-check George Orwell's essay, "Politics and the English Language."[249]

It's not only preference for the positive that prompted this post. Among Jacques Ellul's warnings about propaganda is an alert to what he called social propaganda. This most powerful propaganda drives automatic behavior, triggered from the assumptions and norms wrapped within the context and language that we swim in every day. Even if you're not perturbed about the impact of all these "nots" not-not-negating us into nothingness or worse, media bullhorns that repeat foul fantasies and pretense just perpetuate the mind warp first intended.

Anyway, please consider that a great many people are just plain tired of hearing all the swamp talk of pretenders repeated. Surely, it's time to find a better way to call out the putrid and the puerile? How about perorating the promising? Now there's a prospect!

A pundit is supposed to be, and is often paid to be, well, better–with an opinion to share, with perspective and precision. So, please, can this include putting a stop to promoting drivel?

| *January 13, 2022*

67

It's the PROPAGANDA, Stu***

Today's message is to the media (and all of us, really). Here are the delusions.

"I get personal tweets…" – along with some multi-million others!

"The stock market is up…" – this 47% of the population now own the national debt pumped into the financial markets.

"THEY will take it all off you…" – the biggest fear of all…

In the old days, when my father was selling milking separators to dairy farmers, the farmer had a three-legged chair to sit on while milking the cows. It had three legs, so it stood firmly on any uneven ground.

Three propaganda assaults still work to milk us, apparently. With what flows from each assault spreading like a virus, or to mix figurative language more, like Triffids (could be worth looking this one up). The propagandist counts on your engagement with one or other of the viral "news" flows, while propagating another… and throwing at you the fertilizers of outrage, exaggeration, and repetition. If you're tantalized by such tractor-beams, as pictured in my previous blog, shame on you.

For counterpropaganda, three-legged chairs work too. How about:

1. IGNORE manufactured outrages.

2. Trumpet reality.

3. Advance and repeat what matters to people: **health, shelter, food, safety,** and **freedom.**

Out of these five life positives, surely you can pick three to focus on. At the very least, you'll be in touch with reality and, who knows, when you talk with someone else about what's real, you might help someone else live a little better.

If this is starting to sound like a message with Dick and Dora in a grade-school reading class, it is. You see, I'm willing to IGNORE another successful propagandist who made millions telling you to always flatter

68

your audience. The propagandist knows you will obsess about lies, hyperbole, and insecurities. Don't let it keep happening–it's up to you.

Fact is, the jig is up. Just tell the truth, without quixotically tilting at the propagandist's fantasies. Simple, direct truth hurts the propagandist. Of course, you must keep choosing what really matters to "we, the people"– see "3" above.

Who has the smarts and discipline to build a new three-legged chair?

| *September 15, 2020*

Rip Van Who?

Do you sometimes wish you'd fallen into a long sleep early in 2020 like the fabled Rip Van Winkle? Look around and you will find some people did.

When you encounter anyone like Rip, it's best to be careful. Rip didn't understand much when he met the silent ghosts of Henry Hudson's crew playing a game of nine-pins in the Catskill Mountains. He didn't ask who they were or how they knew his name. He did get their magic purple liquor when he imbibed it, putting him to sleep. It worked well for him to miss the American Revolutionary War.

So, chances are that if you're on an evening or early morning walk trying to social distance from the joggers and dog-walkers, or wherever, when you find someone sleeping or sleepwalking through the twenty-first century, this person won't get much about the present reality either.

There are people to shake awake still. Ever since memory, the USA has yet to turn out the higher percentages of voters recorded in some countries. The powerful way to do this is to get out the vote person-to-person, door-to-door, with facemasks on (not just by phone or the even weaker, other types of social media).

Meantime, to out-think and out-do the propagandist, George Orwell (1946), Vance Packard (1957), Jacques Ellul (1962), and a host of others have provided us with ways to deal with the continuous propaganda that often numbs the "sleepers," and all of us.

For example, Jacques Ellul named the counter actions you can take against a continuous propaganda onslaught.

1. Challenge any propaganda targeting our pre-existing attitudes AND reassert our beliefs in **honesty, justice, temperance, courage,** and **wisdom**—and our desire to live in a society that enables **health, jobs, shelter, food, safety, freedom,** with any bad actor held **accountable.**

2. Highlight the harm to people by those using *anti*-democratic actions to deny **healthcare, jobs, safety, postal services,** etc. AND say exactly what should happen instead.

3. Reassert the rightness of **facts**, positively and specifically (without naming the lie or the liar, to avoid being a megaphone for the corrupt).

4. Keep repeating what is **right** (propaganda decays over time, especially when crowded out of the public communication channels).

Oh, and as George Orwell urged about any verbal refuse, be sure to call out and **mock the foreign propaganda** that misses our culture. As we saw in a previous blog post, this is easy when it's half-baked with lots of "tells."

Too many of our fellow "we, the people" might seem to be awake in their sleepwalk, as they continue to be polite about a propagandist. But some have taken years to publicly call a lie a lie. And some in the media still broadcast unfiltered drivel of a propagandist; or, endlessly micro-analyze this nonsense, thereby promoting the nonsense. Maybe they have some dangerously mistaken belief that this serves some purpose of even-handedness, or democratic debate, or advertising sales.

I even heard a federal senator this week say, completely unacceptably, that the shame for the failure of his opponents to act properly was on his opponents. How about what that senator had not accomplished holding them to account? He wasn't elected to be a bystander.

During this *Big Sleep*, with apologies to Raymond Chandler, many **"we, the people"** patiently expected someone else to stop the useless growth of lawyers taking legal actions. Providing employment for lawyers wasn't supposed to be a main outcome of democracy. Yet too many such proceedings continue in multiple, drawn-out, inconclusive actions, instead of anything useful to stop propagandists.

Lookalike despots, autocrats, and wannabe leaders flourish when they are unchecked. There's still time to block and check in workable ways.

One step we can all help with NOW is to personally encourage friends, family, and neighbors to get out the vote.

| *September 29, 2020*

What to Do

A Gary Larson cartoon that a friend recently shared illustrates, by analogy, some of the dilemma the United States faces tackling domestic terrorism.

In the cartoon, four pampered pooches are standing together in a green field. They are looking toward the edge of trees or woods on the left, and behind them is a pull-cart, with one dog in harness to the cart. The cart is stacked with a few large books that are labeled *Domestication*. The pooches are well-groomed and relaxed, with the lead dog standing on hind legs to read aloud from a large open book, also labeled *Domestication*. This optimistic pooch directs the reading from the book toward the woods, where a wolf-pack glares back at the well-mannered dogs, the wolves fixed in their gaze upon the dogs, and poised for attack, clearly anticipating lunch.

Putting aside the visual exaggeration the cartoonist uses to create the comic, the dilemma remains that "we the people" (also known as "lunch") lack a playbook to handle effectively much less to domesticate propagandists—who ruthlessly wield propaganda as a weapon. The propagandists' onslaughts of delusional, destabilizing, distracting, and frequently disgustingly offensive words and images help distort the attention, actions, beliefs, and social values of each of us and our fellow citizens.

And wouldn't it be a good thought to have some ways to address the real and present threats of domestic terrorists committed to destroying democracy? Especially since mainstream and social media so frequently megaphone the propagandist rants and outrage, thereby assisting the efforts to undermine democracy!

It was more than two decades ago, on the day after 9/11 with a dozen bomb alerts on just that one day, that my wife wisely and sadly said this would change the country forever. Soon afterwards, to handle the threat from foreign terrorism, domestically we all built practices to lessen risk.

But it was two years ago that a neighbor wanted to *help fight the coup*. This then-odd comment was stimulated by a domestic wannabe leader's using such words repeatedly in mailings to the neighbor and so many others. I knew then we were at the beginning of a very different reality.

Domestic terrorists have used age-old emotional appeals, such as fear of "others" or an array of desires... for recognition, for virility, for accomplishment or for belonging, to strengthen connection with adherents and to acquire new followers for the propagandist's worldview.

Unfortunately, as a society, we are well primed to tolerate and respond to propaganda processes, thanks to generations of political and commercial propagandists working us over. For example, perhaps we think of rumor and fashion as two very different realities that we live with. Yet they are very similar in how potently and quickly each spread and stimulate automatic responses. As Jacques Ellul pointed out, rumor and fashion are forms of propaganda; it's just that for self-interest and in the interests of commerce, we allow fashion a more friendly connotation.

Fads of fashion are spread by *ad populum* appeals, advancing a herd-mentality, especially when supported by advertising campaigns. Just one odd example was the now, little-seen yo-yo. This toy, for anyone not familiar with it, consists of small discs joined by an axle spinning at the end of a piece of string, and was featured as far back as 440 BC on a Greek vase.[250] The toy's popularity has waxed and waned over the centuries. From the 1960s, the yo-yo saw a comeback campaign, with a series of television advertisements. It was also used to help sell otherwise unrelated products, as yo-yo dexterous performers toured the world's schools and fairgrounds; and, by the way, promoted products.

These folks displayed skill we wanted to emulate, by delivering amazing tricks with these spinning disks at the end of a piece of string, from the basic "walk-the-dog," which every self-respecting schoolkid might master, to "around-the-world," "rock-the-cradle," and other more elaborate tricks that only the truly competent could tackle after much practice.

All this seemed fairly harmless. It was certainly less immediately dangerous than the physical harm dealt out in some enduringly fashionable contact sports. Yes, fashion is quite the driver of a range of behaviors, including the banal, like hula-hoops, emoji, and the assigning of "likes."

The problem that occurs for "we the people" is when the propagandist, whether commercial or cult-promoting, can find from among all the possible responses that we might make, a relational response that connects us to the propagandist's objective. In other words, we, the propagandized give ourselves over to automatic response to what's said by the propagandist about what's going on around us.

Or, putting this into pulp-talk, when anyone enters that zombie-zone, even someone silently scorning the propagandist or related conspiracy theorists or partisan politicians and pundits, that person becomes a participant in the propagandist's play. A more engaged level in the zombie-zone is when you spend energy on criticizing the propagandist. This usually requires repeating and therefore promoting the propagandist's name and some foolishness or dogma, while making the criticism. Maybe more importantly, it also means you're wasting your time in the propagandist's alternative reality, taking you away from real reality.

In his comprehensive and nuanced book *Propaganda*, Elull concluded by illustrating where propaganda could fail. He implied ways to mount counterattacks, to diminish the impact of propaganda, as I've outlined in other blog posts. The strategies he describes are potent, as are the recommendations more recently in the work of Randal Marlin, so well-grounded in the wisdom of both Ellul and Orwell. All these writers have serious value in these times. Each helps to build further principles and techniques for the practical dismantling of propaganda.

It's good that many school curricula have increasingly included ways to identify and counter propaganda techniques. Many incorporate simple approaches for dismissing the inane emotional fallacies of much advertising; but more and broader efforts are needed.

For example, further strengthening is needed more widely of efforts to teach writing through a problem-solving approach, to advance writing as thinking. For some insights on this, do take a look at former colleague, Roslyn Petelin's interview of Professor David Crystal in 2014 (on YouTube). Crystal raised concern about the absence of grammar from most writing classrooms from the 1960s up until the 1990s, which, as Petelin pointed out, Professor John Frow called "a calamity."[251] Hard to figure how one's supposed to write thoughtfully without a workable knowledge of grammar. Whatever fashion drove this impulse might periodically still need dismantling.

In relation to the domestic terrorists in the United States, it's a reasonable start to keep calling terrorists what they are and to keep calling out lies or "the big lie," while prosecuting illegal behaviors. We do also need to get beyond these first stages and address the systemic challenges though. What will we do to -

* Enhance feelings of belonging in civil society among the propagandist's targets?

* Defuse the impact of rumor that occurs through social media and otherwise, which gains power, as Ellul noted, "...the more the objective fact loses importance and the more the rumor is believed by the multitudes who adhere to it"?[252]

* Nurture a variety of viewpoints through stepped-up "conversation and dialogue… [that is] open" as Ellul urged—to sharpen doubts about formulaic comments, and lessen the likelihood of responding to a propagandist?[253]

* Intercept the spontaneous responses to a propagandist—before any of these become learned responses connected to the propagandist's objective?[254]

Brainwashing seeks to weaken independent thought and absorb the individual into the mass. Ellul pointed out that propaganda more broadly also aims to eliminate individualizing factors. He warned that: "At the moment when the attitudes learned by propaganda begin to prevail… [people] …become collective, and the propagandist who has taught them can then calculate more easily what a given stimulus will elicit from them."[255]

Our better future will be found through the vigor of our strengthening truly individual thought.

| *February 24, 2021*

NOTES

Front Pages

1. Lewis, Sinclair (2014), *It Can't Happen Here*, New York: Signet, p. 359 [1st published 1935]
2. Lewandowsky, Stephan and John Cook (2020), *The Conspiracy Theory Handbook*, p. 3, https://cssn.org/wp-content/uploads/2020/12/Conspiracy-Theory-Handbook-Stephan-Lewandowsky.pdf
3. Wilson, Anna, Seb Wilkes, Yayoi Teramoto, and Scott Hale (2023), "Multimodal Analysis of Disinformation and Misinformation," *Royal Society Open Science*, 10: 230964, p. 3, https://doi.org/10.1098/rsos.230964
4. Cambridge online dictionary, "Fake News" (2018), https://dictionary.cambridge.org/us/dictionary/english/fake-news
5. Molina, Maria D., S. Shyam Sundar, Thai Le, and Dongwon Lee (2021), "'Fake News' Is Not Simply False Information: A Concept Explication and Taxonomy of Online Content," *American Behavioral Science*, 65(2), pp. 180-212, https://doi.org/10.1177/0002764219878224
6. Simchon, Almog, Matthew Edwards, and Stephan Lewandowsky (2024), "The Persuasive Effects of Political Microtargeting in the Age of Generative AI," *PNAS Nexus*, January 29, p. 35, https://doi.org/10.1093/pnasnexus/pgae035, quoting House of Commons, U.K. Parliament (2019), *Digital, Culture, Media and Sport Committee, Disinformation and "fake news:" Final Report*, Technical Report
7. Wilson, Wilkes, Teramoto, and Hale, p. 3
8. Marlin, Randal (2013), *Propaganda and the Ethics of Persuasion*, Peterborough, ON: Broadview, p. 12
9. Malkopoulou, Anthoula and Benjamin Moffitt (2023), "How Not to Respond to Populism," *Comparative European Politics*, March 10, https://doi.org/10.1057/s41295-023-00341-9

Introduction

10. Paine, Thomas (1997), *Common Sense*, Mineola, NY: Dover, p. 51 [1st published 1776]
11. Paine, p. 2
12. Paine, pp. 52-53
13. Ressa, Maria (2022), *How to Stand Up to a Dictator: The Fight for Our Future*, New York: Harper
14. Ressa, p. 32

15. Ressa, p. 179
16. Ressa, p. 185
17. Ressa, p. 248
18. Ressa, p. 253
19. Ressa, p. 258
20. Ressa
21. Snyder, Timothy (2017), *On Tyranny: Twenty Lessons from the Twentieth Century,* New York: Tim Duggan
22. Snyder, p. 83
23. Snyder, p. 99
24. Snyder, p. 111
25. Snow, Nancy (2007), "Media, Terrorism, and the Politics of Fear," *Media Development,* 3, pp. 21-22

1. Are We Ready?

26. Franklin, Benjamin (1722), "Silence DoGood, No. 8 – To the Author of the *New-England Courant*," *The New-England Courant,* July 9
27. _____ (2023), List of elections worldwide in 2024, Wikipedia
28. Collins, Philip (2017a), *When They Go Low, We Go High*, London: 4th Estate, p. 213; Collins, Philip (2017b), 'The Art of Political Speech', Leith, Sam (interviewer), *The Spectator–podcast,* 25 October
29. Lewandowsky, Stephan, Ullrich K.H. Ecker, John Cook, Sander van der Linden, Jon Roozenbeek, and Naomi Oreskes (2023), "Misinformation and the Epistemic Integrity of Democracy," *Current Opinion in Psychology,* 54:101711, October 19, pp. 1-7, [Note: "wisdom of the crowd…Dating back to the 18th century, Condorcet's Jury Theorem has provided mathematical justification for majority-rule voting by showing that collectively, members of a group who have imperfect but above-chance information about competing alternatives are more likely to choose the 'correct' alternative than any one member of the group." p. 2]
30. Claassen, Christopher and Pedro C. Magalhães (2023), "Public Support for Democracy in the United States Has Declined Generationally," *Public Opinion Quarterly,* p. 10
31. Lewandowsky, Ecker, Cook, Van der Linden, Roozenbeek, and Oreskes, p. 1
32. The term "firehose of falsehood" is associated with current Russian tactics, described as "the 'four Ds' : **dismiss** the critic, **distort** the facts, **distract** from the issue, and **dismay** the audience (Lucas & Nimmo 2015), in Paul, Christopher and Miriam Matthews (2020), "Defending against Russian Propaganda," Baines, Paul, Nicholas O'Shaughnessy, and Nancy Snow (Eds.) (2020), *The Sage Handbook of Propaganda,* Thousand Oaks, CA: Sage, pp. 288-289; suggestions for "Defending against Propaganda," pp. 293-298
33. Bolt, Neville (2020), "Propaganda of the Deed and Its Anarchist Origins," in Baines, O'Shaughnessy, and Snow, pp. 3-21
34. Woolley, Samuel C. and Howard, Philip N. (2019), *Computational Propaganda: Political Parties, Politicians and Political Manipulation on Social Media,* Oxford: Oxford University Press, p. 243; Shaffer, Kris (2019), *Data Versus Democracy: How Big Data Algorithms Shape Opinions and Alter the Course of History,* New York: Apress/Springer Science + Business Media, pp. 114-115
35. Miller, Rodney G. (2021), "Thylacine," Word to the wise blog post, November 1
36. Gabis, Stanley T. (1978), "Political Secrecy and Cultural Conflict: A Plea for Formalism," *Administration and Society,* 10(2), August, pp. 139-175

37. See: Baines, O'Shaughnessy, and Snow; Ellul, Jacques (1965), *Propaganda: The Formation of Men's Attitudes,* New York: Knopf; Hobbs, Renee (2020), *Mind Over Media: Propaganda Education for a Digital Age,* New York: W.W. Norton; Jowett, Garth S. and Victoria O'Donnell (2019), 7th edn, *Propaganda and Persuasion,* Thousand Oaks, CA: Sage; Lewandowsky and Cook (2020) [see URL in bibliography]; Marlin (2013); Pomerantsev, Peter (2019), *This Is NOT Propaganda: Adventures in the War Against Reality,* London: Faber and Faber; Sproule, J. Michael (1994), *Channels of Propaganda,* Bloomington, IN: EDINFO Press and ERIC Clearinghouse

2. Can We Stop Whistling in the Wind?

38. Orwell, George (2009), "Propaganda and Demotic Speech," in Packer, George (Ed.), *All Art is Propaganda,* New York: Mariner, p. 231 [1st published in *Persuasion,* Summer Quarter, 1944, 2, No.2]
39. Alekseev, Andrey, Oleg Gurov, Alexander Segal, and Andrey Sheludyakov (2023), "Ideas as Infections: Introduction to the Problematics of Cognitive Metaparasitism," *Epistema,* 1, [explores the dynamics of metaparasites, defined as information designed to manipulate or deceive]
40. Orwell, George (1972), "The Principles of Newspeak," *Nineteen Eighty-Four,* Harmondsworth: Penguin, pp. 241-251 [1st published 1949]
41. Fallon, Peter K. (2022), *Propaganda 2.1: Understanding Propaganda in the Digital Age,* Eugene, OR: Cascade, p. 95
42. _____ (2020), "Propaganda," *Merriam-Webster Dictionary,* merriam-webster.com/dictionary/propaganda
43. Ellul (1965), p. 256
44. Kellen, Konrad, "Introduction," in Ellul (1965), p. vii
45. Ellul (1965), p. 20
46. Lerner, D. (1972), "Effective Propaganda," in Lerner, D. (Ed.), *Propaganda in War and Crisis,* New York: Arno, p. 346
47. Baines, O'Shaughnessy, and Snow, p. xxv
48. Taylor, P. M. (2002), "Strategic Communications or Democratic Propaganda?" *Journalism Studies,* 3, 3, pp. 437-441; Kiss, Peter A. (2023), "Russian Strategic Communication Operations in Support of Strategic Objectives in the Russo-Ukrainian War," November 23; Murphy, Dennis M. and James F. White (2007), "Propaganda: Can a Word Decide a War?," *The US Army War College Quarterly: Parameters 37,* 3, pp. 15-27 [briefly reviews some limitations on countering propaganda in the United States.]
49. Jowett and O'Donnell (2019), pp. 2-7; Marlin (2013), pp. 4-13; Steinfatt, Thomas M. (1979), "Evaluating Approaches to Propaganda Analysis," *ETC: A Review of General Semantics,* 36(2), Summer, pp.159-162
50. Bennett, Beth S. and Sean Patrick O'Rourke (2006), "A Prolegomenon to the Future Study of Rhetoric and Propaganda: Critical Foundations," in Jowett, Garth S. and Victoria O'Donnell (Eds.), *Readings in Propaganda and Persuasion: New and Classic Essays,* Thousand Oaks, CA: Sage, p. 67; see also - Chomsky, Noam (1989) *Necessary Illusions in Democratic Societies,* Boston, MA: South End Press
51. Jowett and O'Donnell (2019), p. 6
52. Ellul (1965), p. 27
53. Ellul (1965), p. xvii
54. Ellul (1965), p. 240

55. Ellul (1965), p. 29
56. Ellul (1965), p. 208
57. Marlin (2013), p. 12
58. Ellul (1965), p. 26
59. Stanley, Jason (2015), *How Propaganda Works,* Princeton: Princeton University Press, p. 5
60. Ellul (1965), p. 312
61. Kellen, in Ellul (1965), p. v-vi
62. Orwell, George (1981), "Politics and the English Language," *A Collection of Essays,* Orlando, FL: Harcourt, p. 156-171 [1st published 1946]
63. Orwell (1972), pp. 241-251
64. Orwell, George (1977), *Animal Farm,* New York: Signet [1st published 1945]
65. Snyder, p. 17
66. Snyder, p. 18
67. Sayers, Dorothy L. (1948), *The Lost Tools of Learning: Paper Read at a Vacation Course in Education, Oxford, 1947,* London: Methuen, p. 4

3. Understanding Propaganda

68. Hamilton, Alexander (1787), *The Federalist,* Number 8, November 20
69. Ellul, Jacques (2006), "The Characteristics of Propaganda," in Jowett and O'Donnell, p. 22
70. Ellul (2006), p. 23
71. Ellul (1965), p. 87
72. Chomsky, Noam (1993), *Language and Thought,* Kingston, RI: Moyer Bell, p. 21
73. Sless, David and Ruth Shrensky (2023), *A New Semiotics: An Introductory Guide for Students,* London and New York: Routledge, p. 46
74. Sless and Shrensky, p. 48
75. Sless and Shrensky, p. 144
76. _____ (1978), "Distortions of Political Language," *Washington Post,* November 21
77. Toler, Aric (2017), "Most Common Way that Fake News Spreads Is from Laziness," STOPFAKE.ORG, https://www.stopfake.org/en/most-common-way-that-fake-news-spreads-is-from-laziness-aric-toler-bellingcat/
78. Ellul (1965), p. xvii; Snyder, p. 17
79. Esposito, Nicholas J. and Leroy H. Pelton (1971), "Review of the Measurement of Semantic Satiation," *Psychological Bulletin,* 75, pp. 330-346; Black, S.R. (2003), "Review of Semantic Satiation," in Shohov, S.P. (Ed.), *Advances in Psychology Research,* 26, Nova Science Publishers, pp. 63-74
80. Marlin, Randal (1984), "The Rhetoric of Action Description: Ambiguity in Intentional Reference," *Informal Logic,* 6, 3, p. 28
81. Collins, Philip (2017a), p. 78
82. Miller, Rodney G. (2022), *Australians Speak Out: Persuasive Language Styles,* Albany, NY: Parula, p. 92
83. Turnbull, Nick (2017), "Political Rhetoric and Its Relationship to Context: A New Theory of the Rhetorical Situations, the Rhetorical and the Political," *Critical Discourse Studies,* XXX, p. 14
84. Ellul (1965), pp. 293-294
85. Wanless, Alicia and Michael Berk (2022), "Participatory Propaganda: The Engagement of Audiences in the Spread of Persuasive Communications," in Herbert, David and Stefan Fisher (Eds.), *Social Media and Social Order,* De Gruyter Open Poland

4. Neutralize Propaganda

86. Ellul (1965), p. 6
87. Snow, Nancy (2013), *Truth Is the Best Propaganda: Edward R. Murrow's Speeches in the Kennedy Years,* Minerva, NY: Minerva Press; Silina, Maria (2022), "Russia's Feminists Are Protesting the War and Its Propaganda with Stickers, Posters, Performance and Graffiti," *The Conversation,* April 7; Maddow, Rachel (2023), *Prequel: An American Fight Against Fascism,* Crown: New York
88. Wood, Tim (2021), "Propaganda, Obviously: How Propaganda Analysis Fixates on the Hidden and Misses the Conspicuous," *Harvard Kennedy School Misinformation Review,* 2(1), April 8
89. Abrams, M. (1964), "Opinion Polls and Party Propaganda," *Public Opinion Quarterly,* 28, Spring, pp. 13-19
90. Ellul (1965), p. 184
91. Ellul (1965), p. 186
92. Miller, Rodney G. (2020), "It's Time for Plain Talk," Word to the wise blog post, June 25
93. Ellul (1965), p. 6
94. _____ (2023), *Morning Joe,* MSNBC broadcast, December
95. United States Census Bureau (2023), *At Height of Pandemic, More Than 51% of People Age 16 and Over Helped Neighbors, More Than 23% Formally Volunteered,* January 25
96. Dascal Marcelo (2017), "Types of Polemics and Types of Polemical Moves," in Cmerjrkova, Svetla, Jana Hoffmanova, Olga Mullerova, Olga M. Lleroy (Eds.), *Dialoganalyse VI/1: Referate de 6. Argbeitstagung, Prag 1996,* Berlin/Boston: Walter de Gruyter GmbH, pp. 21-22
97. Pradelle, Alexaine, Sabine Mainbourg, Steeve Provencher, Emmanuel Massy, Guillaume Grenet, Jean-Christophe Lega (2024), "Deaths Induced by Compassionate Use of Hydroxychloroquine during the First COVID-19 Wave: An Estimate," *Biomedicine & Pharamacotherapy,* 171, Online January 2
98. Constructive Institute (2024), *Why Constructive Journalism?* Website, https://constructiveinstitute.org/why/
99. Pomerantsev, p. 239
100. Ellul (1965), pp. 294-296

5. Counter *Anti*-democracy!

101. Russell, Bertrand (1976), *The Impact of Science on Society,* London: Unwin, p. 72 [1st edition, 1952]
102. Bakir, Vian, Eric Herring, David Miller, and Piers Robinson (2019), "Lying and Deception in Politics," in Meibauer, Jörg (Ed.), *The Oxford Handbook of Lying,* New York: Oxford University Press, p. 540
103. Van der Linden, Sander (2023), *Foolproof: Why Misinformation Infects Our Minds and How to Build Immunity,* New York: W.W. Norton, pp. 275-276
104. Ben-Ghiat, Ruth (2021), *Strongmen: Mussolini to the Present,* New York: W.W. Norton
105. Ellul (1965), p. 256
106. Malkopoulou and Moffitt
107. Malkopoulou and Moffitt
108. Ellul (1965), p. 26
109. Marlin, Randal (2021), "Dynamic Tension for Pandemic Times," *Current Drift,* 10 May, IJES Elul Society, ellul.org/current-drift/dynamic-tension-for-pandemic-times/

110. Kovač, Milan (2022), "Visual Propaganda in the Maya Proto-Writing Period: The Example of Stucco Frieze from Palace H-Sub 2, Uaxactun, Guatemala," pp. 211-32, in Hubina, Miloš and Francis S. M. Chan (Eds.) (2022), *Communicating the Sacred: Varieties of Religious Marketing,* New York: Peter Lang, p. 211

111. Kovač, p. 211

112. Kovač, p. 211

113. Jowett and O'Donnell (2019), p. 51

114. Schiffrin, Anya (2018), "Fighting Disinformation with Media Literacy—in 1939," *Columbia Journalism Review,* October, 10; Schiffrin, Anya (2022), "Fighting Disinformation in the 1930s: Clyde Miller and the Institute for Propaganda Analysis," *International Journal of Communication,* 16, pp. 3715-3741

115. Ridge, Hannah M. (2023), "The d-word: Surveying Democracy in America," *Democratization,* 30(8), December 5

116. Hanson, Russel (1985), *The Democratic Imagination in America: Conversations with Our Past,* Princeton: Princeton University Press, pp. 23-24

117. Teubert, Wolfgang (2019), "The Citizen Caught Between Dialogue, Bureaucracy," in Paige, Ruth, Beatrix Busse and Nina Nørgaard (Eds.), *Rethinking Language, Text and Context: Interdisciplinary Research in Stylistics in Honour of Michael Toolan,* Abingdon: Routledge, p. 312

118. Chomsky, Noam (1988), *Language and Problems of Knowledge: The Managua Lectures,* Cambridge: Massachusetts Institute of Technology, p. 135

119. Kellen, in Ellul (1965), p. vi-vii; Ellul (1965), p. 15

120. Ellul (1965), p. 94-95

121. Neylan, Julian, Mikey Biddlestone, Jon Roozenbeek, and Sander van der Linden (2023), "How to 'Inoculate' against Multimodal Misinformation: A Conceptual Replication of Roozenbeek and Van der Linden (2020), *Scientific Reports,* 13, 18273; Van der Linden (2023)

122. Collins, Philip (2017a), p. 338

123. Collins (2017a), p. 341

124. Collins (2017a), p. 337

125. Collins (2017a), p. 338

126. Kellen, in Ellul (1965), p. vi; Ellul (1965), pp. 70-79

127. Gibson, Walker T. (1966), *Tough, Sweet and Stuffy,* Bloomington: University of Indiana Press, pp. 115-134 [Note: Gibson developed his "instrument" largely to illustrate what language features might suggest colloquial conversation. He acknowledges its limited development, with the tongue-in-cheek name as a "Model-T style machine." His categories of language types "tough/sweet/stuffy" are idiosyncratic. Gibson also acknowledges a defect that, while identifying mixtures in style, the scores do not discriminate between the dreary and the artful.]

128. Ellul (1965), pp. 79-84

129. Ellul (1965), pp. 84-87

130. Ellul (1965), p. 85

131. Mareš, Miroslav and Petra Mlejnková (2021), "Propaganda and Disinformation as a Security Threat," in Gregor, Miloš and Petra Mlejnková (Eds.), *Challenging Online Propaganda and Disinformation in the 21st Century,* Cham, Switzerland: Springer Nature/Palgrave Macmillan, p. 89

132. Fister, Barbara (2023), "Standing Up for the Truth: The Place of Libraries in the Public Sphere," Blog, June 14; Benkler, Yochai, Robert Faris, and Hal Roberts (2018), *Network Propaganda: Manipulation, Disinformation, and Radicalization in American Politics,* New York: Oxford

University Press; Tripodi, Francesca Bolla (2022), *The Propagandist's Playbook: How Conservative Elites Manipulate Search and Threaten Democracy*, New Haven: Yale University Press

133. After an aphorism from a United States postage stamp. The original: "A Public that Reads: A Root of Democracy" indicates the continued concern for literacy as an integral part of the democratic process.

6. ANTI-propaganda Action

134. Sayers, p. 30
135. Simchon, Edwards, and Lewandowsky
136. Ellul (1965), p. 240
137. Kouper, Inna (2022), "Information Practices of Resistance during the 2022 Russian Invasion of Ukraine," *Proceedings of the Association for Information Science and Technology*, 59(1), October 29-November1, pp. 157-168
138. Kepe, Marta and Alyssa Demus (2023), *Resisting Russia: Insights into Ukraine's Civilian-Based Actions During the First Four Months of the War in 2022*, Santa Monica, CA: Rand Corporation, pp. 12-14 and p. 49; Jolley, Daniel and Karen M. Douglas (2017), "Prevention is Better than Cure: Addressing Anti-vaccine Conspiracy Theories," *Journal of Applied Social Psychology*, 47(8), pp. 459-469; Lewandowsky and Cook (2020)
139. Roozenbeek, Jon, Eileen Culloty, and Jane Suiter (2023), "Countering Misinformation: Evidence, Knowledge Gaps, and Implications of Current Interventions," *European Psychologist*, 28(3), July 14; Ziemer, Carolin-Theresa and Tobias Rothmund (2024), "Psychological Underpinnings of Misinformation Countermeasures," *Journal of Media Psychology*, January 23; Courchesne, Laura, Julia Ilhardt, and Jacob N. Shapiro (2021), "Review of Social Science Research on the Impact of Countermeasures against Influence Operations," *Harvard Kennedy School Misinformation Review*, September 13164
140. Bateman, Jon and Dean Jackson (2024), *Countering Disinformation Effectively: An Evidence-Based Policy Guide*, Washington, DC: Carnegie Endowment for International Peace, pp. 1-8; Smith, Zhanna Malekos (2020), "Part II: How the Information Environment is Testing the Mettle of Liberal Democracies," in *Burnt by the Digital Sun*, Washington, DC: Center for Strategic and International Studies, pp. 9-16; Piskorska, Galyna, Daria Ryzhova, and Anatoly Yakovets (2023), "Joint Efforts of the Media, Civil Society, and the State to Counter Russian Disinformation," *International Journal of Innovative Technologies in Social Science*, 3(39); Teperik, Dmitri, Solvita Denisa-Liepniece, Dalia Bankauskaitė, and Kaarel Kullamaa (2022), *Resilience Against Disinformation: A New Baltic Way to Follow?* Estonia: International Centre for Defence and Security
141. Paul, Christopher and Miriam Matthews (2016), *The Russian "Firehose of Falsehood" Propaganda Model: Why It Might Work and Options to Counter It*, Santa Monica, CA: Rand Corporation; Van der Linden (2023), pp. 174-175 and pp. 244-245
142. Carey, John, Brian Fogarty, Marília Gehrke, Brendan Nyhan, and Jason Reifler (2024), "Prebunking and Credible Source Corrections Increase Election Credibility: Evidence from the U.S. and Brazil
143. Paul and Matthews; Roozenbeek, Culloty, and Suiter
144. Van der Linden, pp. 77-79; Paul and Matthews; Garrett, R. Kelly (2017), "The 'Echo Chamber' Distraction: Disinformation Campaigns Are the Problem Not Audience Fragmentation," *Journal of Applied Research in Memory and Cognition*, 6, pp. 370-376

145. Bolt, Neville (2020), "Propaganda of the Deed and Its Anarchist Origins," in Baines, O'Shaughnessy, and Snow, pp. 3-21
146. Paul and Matthews
147. McQuade, Barbara (2024), *Attack from Within: How Disinformation Is Sabotaging America,* New York: Seven Stories Press, pp. 251-281
148. Ellul (1965); Jowett and O'Donnell (2019)
149. Ellul (1965), p. xii
150. Miller, Rodney G. (2023), "Book Review: A New Semiotics: An Introductory Guide for Students by David Sless & Ruth Shrensky," *Media International Australia,* October 6; see also: Phillips, Whitney (2019), "It Wasn't Just the Trolls: Early Internet Culture, 'Fun,' and the Fires of Exclusionary Laughter," *Social Media + Society,* pp. 1-4; Echeverría, Martin and Frida V. Rodelo (2023), *Political Entertainment in a Post-authoritarian Democracy: Humor and the Mexican Media,* Abingdon: Routledge
151. McCright, A. M. and R. E. Dunlap (2017), "Combatting Misinformation Requires Recognizing Its Types and the Factors That Facilitate Its Spread and Resonance," *Journal of Applied Research in Memory and Cognition,* 6(4), pp. 389-396
152. Kellen, in Ellul (1965), p. v
153. Tsipursky, G. (2017), "Towards a Post-lies Future: Fighting 'Alternative Facts' and 'Post-truth' Politics," *The Humanist,* 77(2), pp. 12-15
154. Kellen, in Ellul (1965), p. v
155. Ellul (1965), p. 52
156. Marlin, Randal (2013), pp. 106-109; also, MacLean, Eleanor O'Donnell (1981), *Between the Lines: How to Detect Bias and Propaganda in the News and Everyday Life,* Montreal: Black Rose Books
157. Marlin (2013), pp. 110-113
158. Schiffrin (2018)
159. Sproule, J. Michael (1997), *Propaganda and Democracy: The American Experience of Media and Mass Persuasion,* Cambridge: Cambridge University Press, p. 177
160. Roozenbeek, Culloty, and Suiter, p. 192
161. Sproule (1997), p. 176
162. Hobbs, Renee and Sandra McGee (2014), "Teaching about Propaganda: An Examination of the Historical Roots of Media Literacy," *Journal of Media Literacy Education,* 6(2), p. 59 and p. 63
163. Karam, Savo (2011), "Truths and Euphemisms: How Euphemisms Are Used in the Political Arena," The Southeastern Asian Journal of English Language Studies, 17(1), pp. 5-17
164. Houston, Philip, Michael Floyd, and Susan Carnicero (2012), *Spy the Lie,* New York: St. Martin's Griffin, pp. 55-72
165. Mann, Samantha (2019), "Lying and Lie Detection," in Meibauer, Jörg (Ed.), *The Oxford Handbook of Lying,* Oxford: Oxford University Press, pp. 408-419; Srour, Camille and Jacques Py (2023), "The General Theory of Deception: A Disruptive Theory of Lie Production, Prevention, and Detection," *Psychological Review,* 130(5), pp. 1289-1309
166. Weigle, Michelle C. (2023), "The Use of Web Archives in Disinformation Research," *arXiv.org,* June
167. Al-Tai, Mohammed Haqi, Bashar M. Nema, and Ali Al-Sherbaz (2023), "Deep Learning for Fake News Detection: Literature Review," *Al-Mustansiriyah Journal of Science,* 34, June 2
168. Sayers, p. 4
169. Fleming, David (2019), "Fear of Persuasion in the English Language Arts," *College English,* 81(6), p. 535

170. Sproule, J. Michael (2001), "Authorship and Origins of the Seven Propaganda Devices: A Research Note," *Rhetoric and Public Affairs,* 4(1), Spring, p. 140

171. Sproule (1994), pp. 1-51

172. Bateman and Jackson, p. 6

173. Mason, Lance E., Daniel G. Krutka, and Jeremy Stoddard (2018), "Media Literacy, Democracy, and the Challenges of Fake News," *Journal of Media Literacy Education,* 10(2), pp. 1-10; Kupiecki, Robert and Agnieszka Legucka (Eds.) (2023), *Disinformation and the Resilience of Democratic Societies,* Warsaw: Polski Institute Spraw Międzynarodowych, note: Bryjka, Filip, "Notes on Detecting and Countering Disinformation," pp. 235-264 and Podemska, Justyna and Piotr Podemski, "Protect Yourself Against Disinformation," pp. 265-285; Moral, Pablo, Guillermo Marco, Julio Gonzalo, Jorge Carrillo-de-Albornoz, and Ivan Gonzalo-Verdugo (2023), "Overview of DIPROMATS 2023: Automatic Detection and Characterization of Propaganda Techniques in Messages from Diplomats and Authorities of World Powers," in *Procesamiento del Lenguaje Natural, Revista,* no 71, Septiembre, pp. 397-407; Ventsel, Andreas, Sten Hansson, Merit Rickberg, and Mari-Liis Madisson (2023), "Building Resilience against Hostile Information Influence Activities: How a New Media Literacy Learning Platform Was Developed for the Estonian Defense Forces," *Armed Forces and Society,* April 18, pp. 1-21

174. Hobbs and McGee, pp. 56-67; Hobbs; Naffi, Nadia, Melodie Charest, Sarah Danis, Laurie Pique, Ann-Louise Davidson, Nicholas Brault, Marie-Claude Bernard, and Sylivie Barma (2023), "Empowering Youth to Combat Malicious Deepfakes and Disinformation: An Experimental and Reflective Learning Experience Informed by Personal Construct Theory," *Journal of Constructivist Psychology,* December 20

175. Media Education Lab, Harrington School of Communication and Media, University of Rhode Island, https://mediaeducationlab.com

176. Educating for American Democracy (2021), *Educating for American Democracy Project,* https://www.educatingforamericandemocracy.org

177. Higgins, Lorraine, Elenore Long, and Linda Flower (2006), "Community Literacy: A Rhetorical Model for Personal and Public Inquiry." *Community Literacy Journal,* 1(1), pp. 8-43

178. Young, Marilyn J., Michael K. Launer, and Curtis C. Austin (1990), "The Need for Evaluative Criteria: Conspiracy Argument Revisited, Argumentation and Advocacy," 26(3), pp. 89-107; Anderson, C.W. (2021), "Propaganda, Misinformation, and Histories of Media Techniques," *Harvard Kennedy School Misinformation Review,* 2(2); Kyriakidou, Maria, Marina Morani, Ceri Hughes (2022), "Audience Understandings of Disinformation: Navigating News Media through a Prism of Pragmatic Scepticism," *Journalism,* 24(11), July 20; Ruffo, Giancarlo, Alfonso Semeraro, Anastasia Giachanou, and Paolo Rosso (2023), "Studying Fake News Spreading Polarization Dynamics, and Manipulation by Bots: A Tale of Networks and Language," *Computer Science Review,* 47, February; Bolin, Göran and Risto Kunelius (2023), "The Return of Propaganda: Historical Legacies and Contemporary Conceptualisations," *Nordic Journal of Media Studies,* 5(1), pp. 1-16; Wilson, Wilkes, Teramoto, and Hale; Hameleers, Michael (2023), "Disinformation as a Context-bound Phenomenon: Toward a Conceptual Clarification Integrating Actors, Intentions and Techniques of Creation and Dissemination," *Communication Theory,* October 23, pp. 1-10; Murphy, Gillian, Constance De Saint Laurent, Megan Reynolds, Omar Aftab, Karen Hegarty, Yuning Sun, and Ciara M. Greene (2023), "What Do We Study When We Study Misinformation? A Scoping Review of Experimental Research (2016-2022)," *Harvard Kennedy School Misinformation Review,* November 15; Lewandowsky, Stephan, Sander van der Linden, and Andy Norman (2024), "Opinion: Disinformation Is the Real Threat to Democracy and Public Health," *Scientific*

American, January 30; April, Tay, Li Qian, Stephan Lewandowsky, Mark J. Hurlstone, Tim Kurz, and Ulrich K. H. Ecker (2024), "Thinking Clearly about Misinformation," *Communications Psychology,* 2(4)

179. Baines, O'Shaughnessy, and Snow, pp. 281-284 and pp. 293-298
180. Baines, O'Shaughnessy, and Snow: Neville Bolt – "Propaganda of the Deed and Its Anarchist Origins" pp. 3-21, Ron Schleifer – "Countering Hamas and Hezbollah Propaganda" pp. 281-284, Christopher Paul and Miriam Matthews – "Defending against Russian Propaganda" pp. 293-298, Charlie Winter and Craig Whiteside – "IS's Strategic Communication Tactics" pp. 569-571 and pp. 573-574, Gabriel Weimann – "The Evolution of Terrorist Propaganda in Cyberspace" pp. 586-590
181. Roozenbeek, Culloty, and Suiter
182. Roozenbeek, Culloty, and Suiter; Compton, Josh, Sander van der Linden, John Cook, and Melisa Basol (2021), "Inoculation Theory in the Post-truth Era: Extant Findings and New Frontiers for Contested Science, Misinformation, and Conspiracy Theories," *Social and Personality Psychology Compass,* 15(6), May 5; Ganapini, Marianna (2023), "Beyond Harm: An Ethical Framework to Tackle Misinformation on Social Media," *arXiv.org,* June 5, Philosophy, Computer Science
183. Hyzen, Aaron and Hilde Van den Bulck (2021), "Conspiracies, Ideological Entrepreneurs and Popular Culture," *Media and Communication,* 9(3), pp. 179-188; Engel, Kristen, Shruti Phadke, and Tanushree Mitra (2023), "Learning from the Ex-Believers: Individuals' Journeys In and Out of Conspiracy Theories Online," *Proceedings of the ACM on Human-Computer Interaction,* 7(CSCW2), #285, October 4, pp. 1-37
184. Hyzen, Aaron (2023), "Propaganda and the Web 3.0: Truth and Ideology in the Digital Age," *Nordic Journal of Media Studies,* 5(1), pp. 50-51
185. Wanless, Alicia and Michael Berk (2020), "Audience Is the Amplifier: Participatory Propaganda," in Baines, O'Shaughnessy, and Snow, pp. 85-104; Wanless and Berk (2022)
186. Baines, O'Shaughnessy, and Snow, p. xxxvii-xxxviii
187. Fritz, Gerd (2010), "Controversies," in Jucker, Andreas and Irma Taavitsainen (Eds.), *Historical Pragmatics,* The Hague: De Gruyter Mouton, pp. 451-455

7. Deflection and Deterrence

188. Proverb attributed to King James I, with equivalent expression in Italy; current version - *No news is good news.*
189. Körner, Robert, Jennifer R. Oberbeck, Erik Körner, and Astrid Schütz (2022), "How the Linguistic Styles of Donald Trump and Joe Biden Reflect Different Forms of Power," *Journal of Language and Social Psychology,* April 12, p. 22
190. Wollaeger, Mark (2013), "Propaganda and Pleasure: From Kracauer to Joyce," in Auerbach, Johnathan and Russ Castronovo (Eds.), *The Oxford Handbook of Propaganda Studies,* New York: Oxford University Press, pp. 280-281
191. Baines, Paul and Nigel Jones (2020), "Countering Fear in Propaganda," in Baines, O'Shaughnessy, and Snow, p. 336
192. Baines and Jones, pp. 343-347; Tannenbaum, Melanie B., Justin Hepler, Rick S. Zimmerman, Lindsey Saul, Samantha Jacobs, Kristina Wilson, and Delores Albarracín (2015), "Appealing to Fear: A Meta-Analysis of Fear Appeal Effectiveness and Theories," *Psychological Bulletin,* 141(6), pp. 1178-1204

193. Phillips; Ecker, Ullrich K. H., Stephan Lewandowsky, Olivia Fenton, and Kelsey Martin (2014), "Do People Keep Believing because They Want to? Preexisting Attitudes and Continued Influence of Misinformation," *Memory and Cognition,* 42(2)

194. Engel, Phadke, and Mitra

195. _____ (2023), *Morning Joe*

196. Michels, Ank and Laurens De Graaf (2017), "Examining Citizen Participation: Local Participatory Policymaking and Democracy Revisited," *Local Government Studies,* 43(6), pp. 875-881; Federal Chancellery of Switzerland (2024), "Cantonal Parliament: Role and Composition," *ch.ch* website

197. Higgins, Long, and Flower (2006), p. 10

198. Robinson, Viviane, Frauke Meyer, Deidre Le Fevre, and Claire Sinnema (n.d.), "The Quality of Leaders's Problem-solving Conversations: Truth-seeking or Truth-claiming?"

199. Zamęcki, Łukasz and Adam Szymański (2023), "Unintentional Democratic Backsliders. 'Evil Always Wins through the Strength of Its Splendid Dupes,'" *Polish Political Science Review,* 11(1), June 30, pp. 40-41

200. Zamęcki and Szymański, p. 25

201. European Commission (2022), *Fighting Disinformation: 2022 Strengthened Code of Practice,* June 16, Brussels: European Union

202. Chen, Alan K. and Justin Marceau (2018), "Developing a Taxonomy of Lies under The First Amendment," *University of Colorado Law Review,* 89, p. 703, for U.S. Federal law governing limits to free speech, as interpreted in the ruling from United States v. Alvarez, 567 U.S. 709 (2012), with discussion of the limited ability to restrict lies, see:
https://supreme.justia.com/cases/federal/us/567/709/

203. Druzin, Bryan H. and Jessica Li (2010), "The Criminalization of Lying: Under What Circumstances, If Any, Should Lies Be Made Criminal?" *The Journal of Criminal Law and Criminology (1973-),* 101(2), pp. 571-572

204. Druzin and Li, p. 562

205. Druzin and Li, p. 563

206. Hoffman, David A. (2006), "The Best Puffery Article Ever," Legal Studies Research Paper Series, Research Paper No. 2006-11, *91 Iowa Law Review 1395,* p. 103

207. Hoffman, p. 145

208. Hoffman, p. 133

209. Brown, Étienne (2019), "'Fake News' and Conceptual Ethics," *Journal of Ethics and Social Philosophy,* 16(2), p. 147

210. Mackie, Chris (2016), "Lessons from Ancient Athens: The Art of Exiling Your Enemies," *The Conversation,* November 22 [Note: Arguably, in the spirit of ostracism is the provision in some democracies for removal from elected office through a citizens' petition and conduct of a successful recall election.]

211. Oral, Uğur (2023), "'Ostracism,' The People's Way of Protecting Democracy from Tyrants in Ancient Athens," *Electronic Journal of Social Sciences,* April 22, 86, p. 659

212. Oral, p. 657

8. Going Forward

213. Ressa, p. 257 and pp. 267-268

214. Galer, Sophia Smith (2023), "The Harm Caused by Dehumanizing Language," *BBC online,* October 23

215. Druzin, Bryan H. and Gregory Gordon (2018), "Authoritarianism and the Internet," *Law & Social Inquiry,* 43(4), p. 27; see also: Herman, Edward S. and Noam Chomsky (1988), *Manufacturing Consent: The Political Economy of the Mass Media,* New York: Pantheon, p. 360; Ressa, p. 43

216. O'Shaughnessy, Nicholas (2017), "Putin, Xi, and Hitler - Propaganda and the Paternity of Pseudo Democracy," *Defense Strategic Communications: The Official Journal of the NATO Strategic Communications Center of Excellence,* 2, Spring, p. 115

217. O'Shaughnessy (2017), pp. 115-130

218. Lifton, Robert Jay (1983), *The Protean Self: Human Resilience in an Age of Fragmentation,* New York: Basic Books, p. 1

219. Snow, Nancy (2020), *Unmasking the Virus: Public Diplomacy and the Pandemic,* Public Diplomacy Council, the Public Diplomacy Association of America, and the USC Annenberg Center for Communications Leadership & Policy, June 9

220. Snow, Nancy E. (Ed.) (2024), *The Self, Civic Virtue, and Public Life,* Abingdon: Routledge, pp. 1-8

221. Higgins, Long, and Flower, pp. 8-43

222. Salaverría, Ramón and Gustavo Cardoso (2023), "Future of Disinformation Studies: Emerging Research Fields," *Professional de la Información,* 32(5), e320525, pp. 1-7; Çela, Erlis (2023), "Examining Journalist's Perception of Fake News and Their Attitude toward Debunking Disinformation," *Studies in Media and Communication,* 11(6), September, pp. 385-397; Farkas, Johan (2022), "News on Fake News: Logics of Media Discourses on Disinformation," *Journal of Language and*; Farkas, Johan (2023), "Fake News in Metajournalistic Discourse," *Journalism Studies,* January 6

223. Brooks, David (2018), "Opinion: The Failures of Anti-Trumpism," *The New York Times,* April 10, p. 27; Lakoff, George (2016), *Understanding Trump,* August, excerpt from *Moral Politics: How Liberals and Conservatives Think,* (3rd edn), Chicago: University of Chicago Press; Pinker, Steven (2006), "Block That Metaphor!" *The New Republic,* October 8 [Pinker observes in relation to Lakoff's approach to "conceptual analysis" that by claiming "conservatives think in terms of direct rather than systemic causation… [he] …seems unaware that conservatives have been making exactly this accusation against progressives for centuries."]

224. Wood

225. McGee, John A. (1929), *Persuasive Speaking,* New York: Scribner's, pp. 268-269 (Appendix C)

226. Rosenberg, Justus (2020), *The Art of Resistance: My Four Years in the French Underground, a Memoir,* New York: Harper Collins

227. Kjeldsen, Jens E., Christian Kock, and Orla Vigsø (2021), "Political Rhetoric in Scandinavia," in Skorgerbø, E., Ø. Ihlen, N.N. Kristensen, and L. Nord (Eds.), *Power, Communication, and Politics in the Nordic Countries,* Gothenburg: Nordicom, University of Gothenburg, pp. 368-369

228. Kjeldsen, Jens E. (2023), "The Practice and Pragmatics of Scandinavian Research in Rhetoric. Audience Studies in Scandinavian Rhetorical Scholarship," *Res Rhetorica,* 10(4), pp. 12-13

229. Briant, Emma Louise (2015), *Propaganda and Counter-terrorism: Strategies for Global Change,* Manchester, UK: Manchester University Press, p. 27

230. Lewandowsky and Cook (2020); Neylan, Biddlestone, Roozenbeek, and Van der Linden; Van der Linden (2023)

231. Orme, Stuart (Director)/Michael Horowitz/IMDbPro (2015), "Trespass," *Foyle's War,* Season 9, Episode 2

232. Ellul (1965), p. 87

233. Ashinoff, Brandon K., Nicholas M. Singletary, Seth C. Baker, and Guillermo Horga (2022), "Rethinking Delusions: A Selective Review of Delusion Research through a Computational Lens," *Schizophr Res.*, July, 245, pp. 23-41; Ariely, Dan (2023), *Misbelief: What Makes Rational People Believe in Irrational Things*, New York: Harper Collins, pp. 139-164

234. Briant, p. 6, citing Ellul, pp. 238-242

235. Zada, John (2021), *Veils of Distortion: How the News Media Warps Our Minds*, Toronto: Terra Incognito, pp. 130-131

236. Zada, p. 126

237. Andersen, Robin and Jonathan Gray (Eds.) (2008), *Battleground the Media, Volume 2 (O-Z)*, Westport, CT: Greenwood, p. 477

238. Zada, pp. 127-128

239. Wilson, Douglas L. (2007), *Lincoln's Sword: The Presidency and the Power of Words*, New York: Vintage, pp. 38-39

240. Zada, p. 125, pp. 10-12 and pp. 125-136

241. Gardiner, Cait, Abby Kiesa, and Alberto Medina (2020), *Youth Volunteering on Political Campaigns*, Center for Information & Research on Civic Learning and Engagement

242. Briant, p. 27

243. Ressa, p. 255

244. Ressa, pp. 253-258

Appendix

245. Miller, Rodney G. (2020–2022), Word to the wise blog posts: *It's Time for Plain Talk* 6/25/20, *Pundit Propaganda* 1/13/22, *It's the Propaganda STU**** 9/15/20, *Rip Van Who?* 9/29/2020, *What to Do* 2/24/2021

246. Sanderson III, Paul G. (2009), *Augustus Saint-Gaudens: Master of American Sculpture*, PBS Documentary, Our Town Films, WNET/Thirteen, September 13

247. Ratcliffe, Susan (2010), *Oxford Dictionary of Quotations by Subject*, Oxford: Oxford University Press, p. 253

248. Orwell (1981), p. 171

249. Orwell (1981), pp. 156-171

250. Madden, Erin (2019) "The Popularization of the Yo-yo," YO-YO–The Mysteries of the Yo-Yo, Fredericksburg, Va.: University of Mary Washington, *WordPress Website*

251. Petelin, Roslyn (2014), *UQx Write101x English Grammar and Style*-Video, St. Lucia, Qld: The University of Queensland, *Website*

252. Ellul (1965), pp. 293-294

253. Ellul (1965), p. 300

254. Ellul (1965), p. 301

255. Ellul (1965), p. 302

BIBLIOGRAPHY

_____ (1978), "Distortions of Political Language," *Washington Post*, November 21, www.washingtonpost.com/archive/politics/1978/11/21/distortions-of-political-language/47d51dc5-cff4-4424-84ea-1931a216ab96/

_____ (2020), "Propaganda," *Merriam-Webster Dictionary*, merriam-webster.com/dictionary/propaganda

_____ (2023), List of elections worldwide in 2024, Wikipedia

_____ (2023), *Morning Joe*, MSNBC broadcast, December

_____ (2024), United States v. Alvarez, 567 U.S. 709 (2012), https://supreme.justia.com/cases/federal/us/567/709/

Abrams, M. (1964), "Opinion Polls and Party Propaganda," *Public Opinion Quarterly,* 28, Spring, pp. 13-19

Alekseev, Andrey, Oleg Gurov, Alexander Segal, and Andrey Sheludyakov (2023), "Ideas as Infections: Introduction to the Problematics of Cognitive Metaparasitism," *Epistema*, 1, https://epistema.jes.su/s0028991-0-1/

Al-Tai, Mohammed Haqi, Bashar M. Nema, and Ali Al-Sherbaz (2023), "Deep Learning for Fake News Detection: Literature Review," *Al-Mustansiriyah Journal of Science*, 34, June 2, https://www.semanticscholar.org/reader/870d37d43ae7e34abc37225905230df91647015e

Anderson, C.W. (2021), "Propaganda, Misinformation, and Histories of Media Techniques," *Harvard Kennedy School Misinformation Review,* 2(2), https://misinforeview.hks.harvard.edu/article/propaganda-misinformation-and-histories-of-media-techniques/

April, Tay, Li Qian, Stephan Lewandowsky, Mark J. Hurlstone, Tim Kurz, and Ulrich K. H. Ecker (2024), "Thinking Clearly about Misinformation," *Communications Psychology,* 2(4), https://doi.org/10.1038/s44271-023-00054-5

Ariely, Dan (2023), *Misbelief: What Makes Rational People Believe in Irrational Things,* New York: Harper Collins

Ashinoff, Brandon K., Nicholas M. Singletary, Seth C. Baker, and Guillermo Horga (2022), "Rethinking Delusions: A Selective Review of Delusion Research through a Computational Lens," *Schizophr Res.,* July, 245, pp. 23-41, https://www.ncbi.nlm.nih.gov/pmc/articles/PMC8413395/

Baines, Paul, Nicholas O'Shaughnessy, and Nancy Snow (Eds.) (2020), *The Sage Handbook of Propaganda,* Thousand Oaks, CA: Sage

Baines, Paul and Nigel Jones (2020), "Countering Fear in Propaganda," in Baines, O'Shaughnessy, and Snow, pp. 336-349

Bakir, Vian, Eric Herring, David Miller, and Piers Robinson (2019), "Lying and Deception in Politics," in Meibauer, Jörg (Ed.), *The Oxford Handbook of Lying*, New York: Oxford University Press, pp. 527-540

Bateman, Jon and Dean Jackson (2024), *Countering Disinformation Effectively: An Evidence-Based Policy Guide*, Washington, DC: Carnegie Endowment for International Peace, https://carnegieendowment.org/files/Carnegie_Countering_Disinformation_Effectively.pdf

Benkler, Yochai, Robert Faris, and Hal Roberts (2018), *Network Propaganda: Manipulation, Disinformation, and Radicalization in American Politics*, New York: Oxford University Press

Ben-Ghiat, Ruth (2021), *Strongmen: Mussolini to the Present*, New York: W.W. Norton

Bennett, Beth S. and Sean Patrick O'Rourke (2006), "A Prolegomenon to the Future Study of Rhetoric and Propaganda: Critical Foundations," in Jowett and O'Donnell, pp. 51-71

Black, S.R. (2003), "Review of Semantic Satiation," in Shohov, S.P. (Ed.), *Advances in Psychology Research*, 26, Nova Science Publishers, pp. 63-74

Bolin, Göran and Risto Kunelius (2023), "The Return of Propaganda: Historical Legacies and Contemporary Conceptualisations," *Nordic Journal of Media Studies*, 5(1), pp. 1-16, https://sciendo.com/article/10.2478/njms-2023-0001

Bolt, Neville (2020), "Propaganda of the Deed and Its Anarchist Origins," Baines, O'Shaughnessy, and Snow, pp. 3-21

Briant, Emma Louise (2015), *Propaganda and Counter-terrorism: Strategies for Global Change*, Manchester, UK: Manchester University Press

Brooks, David (2018), "Opinion: The Failures of Anti-Trumpism," *The New York Times*, April 10, p. 27

Brown, Étienne (2019), "'Fake News' and Conceptual Ethics," *Journal of Ethics and Social Philosophy*, 16(2), pp. 144-154, https://www.jesp.org/index.php/jesp/article/view/648

Bruns, Hendrik, François J. Dessart, Michal Wiktor Krawczyk, Stephan Lewandowsky, Myrto Pantazi, Gordon Pennycook, Philipp Schmid, and Laura Smillie (2023), "The Role of (Trust in) the Source of Prebunks and Debunks of Misinformation. Evidence from Online Experiments in Four EU Countries," OSFPreprints, December 4, pp. 1-48, https://osf.io/preprints/osf/vd5qt

Bryjka, Filip (2023), "Notes on Detecting and Countering Disinformation," in Kupiecki, Robert and Agnieszka Legucka (Eds.), *Disinformation and the Resilience of Democratic Societies*, Warsaw: Polski Instytut Spraw Międzynarodowych pp. 235-264, https://www.researchgate.net/publication/372419503_Disinformation_and_the_Resilience_of_Democratic_Societies

Cambridge online dictionary (2018), "Fake News," https://dictionary.cambridge.org/us/dictionary/english/fake-news

Carey, John, Brian Fogarty, Marília Gehrke, Brendan Nyhan, and Jason Reifler (2024), "Prebunking and Credible Source Corrections Increase Election Credibility: Evidence from the U.S. and Brazil," https://bpb-us-e1.wpmucdn.com/sites.dartmouth.edu/dist/5/2293/files/2024/02/voter-fraud-corrections-e163369556a2d7a4.pdf

Çela, Erlis (2023), "Examining Journalist's Perception of Fake News and Their Attitude toward Debunking Disinformation," *Studies in Media and Communication*, 11(6), September, pp. 385-397

Chen, Alan K. and Justin Marceau (2018), "Developing a Taxonomy of Lies under The First Amendment," *University of Colorado Law Review,* 89, pp. 656-706, https://scholar.law.colorado.edu/cgi/viewcontent.cgi?article=1207&context=lawreview

Chomsky, Noam (1988), *Language and Problems of Knowledge: The Managua Lectures,* Cambridge: Massachusetts Institute of Technology

Chomsky, Noam (1989) *Necessary Illusions in Democratic Societies,* Boston, MA: South End Press

Chomsky, Noam (1993), *Language and Thought,* Kingston, RI: Moyer Bell

Claassen, Christopher and Pedro C. Magalhães (2023), "Public Support for Democracy in the United States Has Declined Generationally," *Public Opinion Quarterly,* Online pp. 1-14, https://doi.org/10.1093/poq/nfad039

Collins, Philip (2017a), *When They Go Low, We Go High: Speeches that Shape the World and Why We Need Them,* London: 4th Estate

Collins, Philip (2017b), 'The Art of Political Speech', Leith, Sam (interviewer), *The Spectator–podcast,* 25 October

Compton, Josh, Sander van der Linden, John Cook, and Melisa Basol (2021), "Inoculation Theory in the Post-truth Era: Extant Findings and New Frontiers for Contested Science, Misinformation, and Conspiracy Theories," *Social and Personality Psychology Compass,* 15(6), May 5, https://compass.onlinelibrary.wiley.com/doi/10.1111/spc3.12602

Constructive Institute (2024), *Why Constructive Journalism?* Website, https://constructiveinstitute.org/why/

Courchesne, Laura, Julia Ilhardt, and Jacob N. Shapiro (2021), "Review of Social Science Research on the Impact of Countermeasures against Influence Operations," *Harvard Kennedy School Misinformation Review,* September 13, https://misinforeview.hks.harvard.edu/article/review-of-social-science-research-on-the-impact-of-countermeasures-against-influence-operations/

Dascal Marcelo (2017), "Types of Polemics and Types of Polemical Moves," in Cmerjrkova, Svetla, Jana Hoffmanova, Olga Mullerova, Olga M. Lleroy (Eds.), *Dialoganalyse VI/1: Referate de 6. Argbeitstagung, Prag 1996,* Berlin/Boston: Walter de Gruyter GmbH, pp. 21-22

Druzin, Bryan H. and Jessica Li (2010), "The Criminalization of Lying: Under What Circumstances, If Any, Should Lies Be Made Criminal?" *The Journal of Criminal Law and Criminology (1973-),* 101(2), pp. 529-573, https://scholarlycommons.law.northwestern.edu/cgi/viewcontent.cgi?httpsredir=1&article=7396&context=jclc

Druzin, Bryan H. and Gregory Gordon (2018), "Authoritarianism and the Internet," *Law & Social Inquiry,* 43(4), pp. 1-31, https://papers.ssrn.com/sol3/papers.cfm?abstract_id=3387445

Echeverría, Martin and Frida V. Rodelo (2023), *Political Entertainment in a Post-authoritarian Democracy: Humor and the Mexican Media,* Abingdon: Routledge

Ecker, Ullrich K. H., Stephan Lewandowsky, Olivia Fenton, and Kelsey Martin (2014), "Do People Keep Believing because They Want to? Preexisting Attitudes and Continued Influence of Misinformation," *Memory and Cognition,* 42(2), https://link.springer.com/article/10.3758/s13421-013-0358-x

Educating for American Democracy (2021), *Educating for American Democracy Project,* https://www.educatingforamericandemocracy.org

Ellul, Jacques (1965), *Propaganda: The Formation of Men's Attitudes,* New York: Knopf

Ellul, Jacques (2006), "The Characteristics of Propaganda," in Jowett and O'Donnell, pp. 1-49

Engel, Kristen, Shruti Phadke, and Tanushree Mitra (2023), "Learning from the Ex-Believers: Individuals' Journeys In and Out of Conspiracy Theories Online," *Proceedings of the ACM on Human-Computer Interaction,* 7(CSCW2), #285, October 4, pp. 1-37, https://dl.acm.org/doi/10.1145/3610076

Esposito, Nicholas J. and Leroy H. Pelton (1971), "Review of the Measurement of Semantic Satiation," *Psychological Bulletin,* 75, pp. 330-346

European Commission (2022), *Fighting Disinformation: 2022 Strengthened Code of Practice,* June 16, Brussels: European Union, https://digital-strategy.ec.europa.eu/en/policies/code-practice-disinformation

Fallon, Peter K. (2022), *Propaganda 2.1: Understanding Propaganda in the Digital Age,* Eugene, OR: Cascade

Farkas, Johan (2022), "News on Fake News: Logics of Media Discourses on Disinformation," *Journal of Language and Politics,* https://doi.org/10.1075/jlp.22020.far

Farkas, Johan (2023), "Fake News in Metajournalistic Discourse," *Journalism Studies,* January 6, https://doi.org/10.1080/1461670X.2023.2167106

Federal Chancellery of Switzerland (2024), "Cantonal Parliament: Role and Composition," *ch.ch* website, https://www.ch.ch/en/political-system/cantons/cantonal-parliament:-role-and-composition/#president-of-the-cantonal-parliament

Fister, Barbara (2023), "Standing Up for the Truth: The Place of Libraries in the Public Sphere," Blog, June 14, https://barbarafister.net/libraries/standing-up-for-the-truth/

Fleming, David (2019), "Fear of Persuasion in the English Language Arts," *College English,* 81(6), pp. 508-541, https://works.bepress.com/david-fleming/31/

Fondren, Elisabeth (2021), "'We Are Propagandists for Democracy': The Institute for Propaganda Analysis' Pioneering Media Literacy Efforts to Fight Disinformation (1937-1942)," *American Journalism,* 38(3), pp. 258-291, https://www.tandfonline.com/doi/full/10.1080/08821127.2021.1950481?scroll=top&need Access=true

Franklin, Benjamin (1722), "Silence DoGood, No. 8 – To the Author of the *New-England Courant,*" *The New-England Courant,* July 9, https://founders.archives.gov/documents/Franklin/01-01-02-0015

Fritz, Gerd (2010), "Controversies," in Jucker, Andreas and Irma Taavitsainen (Eds.), *Historical Pragmatics,* The Hague: De Gruyter Mouton, pp. 451-481, https://www.researchgate.net/publication/255832142_Controversies

Gabis, Stanley T. (1978), "Political Secrecy and Cultural Conflict: A Plea for Formalism," *Administration and Society,* 10(2), August, pp. 139-175, https://doi.org/10.1177/009539977801000202

Galer, Sophia Smith (2023), "The Harm Caused by Dehumanizing Language," *BBC online,* October 23, https://www.bbc.com/future/article/20231030-the-real-life-harm-caused-by-dehumanising-language

Ganapini, Marianna (2023), "Beyond Harm: An Ethical Framework to Tackle Misinformation on Social Media," *arXiv.org,* June 5, https://arxiv.org/abs/2306.02964

Gardiner, Cait, Abby Kiesa, and Alberto Medina (2020), *Youth Volunteering on Political Campaigns,* Center for Information & Research on Civic Learning and Engagement, https://circle.tufts.edu/latest-research/youth-volunteering-political-campaigns

Garrett, R. Kelly (2017), "The 'Echo Chamber' Distraction: Disinformation Campaigns Are the Problem Not Audience Fragmentation," *Journal of Applied Research in Memory and Cognition,* 6, pp. 370-376, https://rkellygarrett.com/wp-content/uploads/2018/07/Garrett-Echo-chamber-distraction.pdf

Gasiorek, Jessika and R. Kelly Aune (2021), *Creating Understanding: How Communicating Aligns Minds,* New York: Peter Lang

Gibson, Walker T. (1966), *Tough, Sweet and Stuffy,* Bloomington: University of Indiana Press

Hameleers, Michael (2023), "Disinformation as a Context-bound Phenomenon: Toward a Conceptual Clarification Integrating Actors, Intentions and Techniques of Creation and Dissemination," *Communication Theory,* October 23, pp. 1-10, https://core.ac.uk/reader/555953303

Hamilton, Alexander (1787), *The Federalist,* Number 8, 20 November, founders.archives.gov/documents/Hamilton/01-04-02-0160

Hanson, Russel (1985), *The Democratic Imagination in America: Conversations with Our Past,* Princeton: Princeton University Press

Harson, Jayson (2024), "Three Critiques of Disinformation (For-Hire) Scholarship: Definitional Vortexes, Disciplinary Unneighborliness, and Cryptonormativity," *Social Meida + Society,* 10(1), January 27, file:///Users/p/Desktop/Three%20Critiques%20of%20Disinformation%20(For-Hire)%20Scholarship:%20Definitional%20Vortexes,%20Disciplinary%20Unneig.html#skipNavigationTo

Herbert, David and Stefan Fisher (Eds.) (2022), *Social Media and Social Order,* De Gruyter Open Poland

Herman, Edward S. and Noam Chomsky (1988), *Manufacturing Consent: The Political Economy of the Mass Media,* New York: Pantheon

Hickey, Walter (2023), *You Are What You Watch: How Movies and TV Affect Everything,* New York: Workman Publishing

Higgins, Lorraine, Elenore Long, and Linda Flower (2006), "Community Literacy: A Rhetorical Model for Personal and Public Inquiry." *Community Literacy Journal,* 1(1), pp. 8-43, doi:10.25148/clj.1.1.009529

Hobbs, Renee and Sandra McGee (2014), "Teaching about Propaganda: An Examination of the Historical Roots of Media Literacy," *Journal of Media Literacy Education,* 6(2), https://files.eric.ed.gov/fulltext/EJ1046525.pdf

Hobbs, Renee (2020), *Mind Over Media: Propaganda Education for a Digital Age,* New York: W.W. Norton, also Media Education Lab, Harrington School of Communication and Media, University of Rhode Island, mediaeducationlab.com

Hoffman, David A. (2006), "The Best Puffery Article Ever," Legal Studies Research Paper Series, Research Paper No. 2006-11, *91 Iowa Law Review 1395,* pp. 101-151, https://papers.ssrn.com/sol3/papers.cfm?abstract_id=887720

Houston, Philip, Michael Floyd, and Susan Carnicero (2012), *Spy the Lie,* New York: St. Martin's Griffin

Hyzen, Aaron and Hilde Van den Bulck (2021), "Conspiracies, Ideological Entrepreneurs and Popular Culture," *Media and Communication,* 9(3), pp. 179-188,

93

https://pdfs.semanticscholar.org/48ce/de9f3c674c2b347cebaae7e0c3cf9e6d6c53.pdf

Hyzen, Aaron (2023), "Propaganda and the Web 3.0: Truth and Ideology in the Digital Age," *Nordic Journal of Media Studies,* 5(1), pp. 49-67, https://sciendo.com/article/10.2478/njms-2023-0004

Jackson, Dean (2017), "Issue Brief: Distinguishing Disinformation from Propaganda, Misinformation, and 'Fake News,'" *National Endowment for Democracy,* October 17, https://www.ned.org/issue-brief-distinguishing-disinformation-from-propaganda-misinformation-and-fake-news/

Jolley, Daniel and Karen M. Douglas (2017), "Prevention is Better than Cure: Addressing Anti-vaccine Conspiracy Theories," *Journal of Applied Social Psychology,* 47(8), pp. 459-469, https://researchportal.northumbria.ac.uk/ws/portalfiles/portal/22352978/Jolley_Douglas_2017_Intervention.pdf

Jowett, Garth S. and Victoria O'Donnell (Eds.) (2006), *Readings in Propaganda and Persuasion: New and Classic Essays,* Thousand Oaks, CA: Sage

Jowett, Garth S. and Victoria O'Donnell (2019), 7th edn, *Propaganda and Persuasion,* Thousand Oaks, CA: Sage

Karam, Savo (2011), "Truths and Euphemisms: How Euphemisms Are Used in the Political Arena," *The Southeastern Asian Journal of English Language Studies,* 17(1), pp. 5-17, http://journalarticle.ukm.my/2043/1/2._3LVol17(1)2011Savo_Karam.pdf

Kepe, Marta and Alyssa Demus (2023), *Resisting Russia: Insights into Ukraine's Civilian-Based Actions During the First Four Months of the War in 2022,* Santa Monica, CA: Rand Corporation, https://www.rand.org/content/dam/rand/pubs/research_reports/RRA2000/RRA2034-1/RAND_RRA2034-1.pdf

Kiss, Peter A. (2023), "Russian Strategic Communication Operations in Support of Strategic Objectives in the Russo-Ukrainian War," November 23, https://www.researchgate.net/publication/375795717_Peter_A_Kiss_Russian_Strategic_Communication_Operations_in_Support_of_Strategic_Objectives_in_the

Kjeldsen, Jens E. (2023), "The Practice and Pragmatics of Scandinavian Research in Rhetoric. Audience Studies in Scandinavian Rhetorical Scholarship," *Res Rhetorica,* 10(4), pp. 10-27, https://www.researchgate.net/publication/377069911_The_practice_and_pragmatics_of_Scandinavian_research_in_rhetoric_Audience_studies_in_Scandinavian_rhetorical_scholarship

Kjeldsen, Jens E., Christian Kock, and Orla Vigsø (2021), "Political Rhetoric in Scandinavia," in Skorgerbø, E., Ø. Ihlen, N.N. Kristensen, and L. Nord (Eds.), *Power, Communication, and Politics in the Nordic Countries,* Gothenburg: Nordicom, University of Gothenburg, pp. 365-383, https://bora.uib.no/bora-xmlui/bitstream/handle/11250/2763090/Kjeldsen%252C%2BKock%2B%2526%2BVigs%25C3%25B8_Political%2Brhetoric%2Bin%2BScandinavia.pdf?sequence=2

Körner, Robert, Jennifer R. Oberbeck, Erik Körner, and Astrid Schütz (2022), "How the Linguistic Styles of Donald Trump and Joe Biden Reflect Different Forms of Power," *Journal of Language and Social Psychology,* April 12, pp. 1-28, https://journals.sagepub.com/doi/full/10.1177/0261927X221085309

Kouper, Inna (2022), "Information Practices of Resistance during the 2022 Russian Invasion of Ukraine," *Proceedings of the Association for Information Science and Technology,* 59(1), October 29-November1, pp. 157-168, https://www.researchgate.net/publication/364530458_Information_Practices_of_Resistance_during_the_2022_Russian_Invasion_of_Ukraine

94

Kovač, Milan (2022), "Visual Propaganda in the Maya Proto-Writing Period: The Example of Stucco Frieze from Palace H-Sub 2, Uaxactun, Guatemala," in Hubina, Miloš and Francis S. M. Chan (Eds.) (2022), *Communicating the Sacred: Varieties of Religious Marketing,* New York: Peter Lang, pp. 211-232

Kupiecki, Robert and Agnieszka Legucka (Eds.) (2023), *Disinformation and the Resilience of Democratic Societies,* Warsaw: Polski Institute Spraw Międzynarodowych, note: Bryjka, Filip, "Notes on Detecting and Countering Disinformation," pp. 235-264 and Podemska, Justyna and Piotr Podemski, "Protect Yourself Against Disinformation," pp. 265-285,
https://www.researchgate.net/publication/372419503_Disinformation_and_the_Resilience_of_Democratic_Societies

Kyriakidou, Maria, Marina Morani, Ceri Hughes (2022), "Audience Understandings of Disinformation: Navigating News Media through a Prism of Pragmatic Scepticism," *Journalism,* 24(11), July 20,
https://journals.sagepub.com/doi/full/10.1177/14648849221114244

Lakoff, George (2016), *Understanding Trump,* August, excerpt from *Moral Politics: How Liberals and Conservatives Think,* (3rd edn), Chicago: University of Chicago Press,
https://press.uchicago.edu/books/excerpt/2016/lakoff_trump.html

Lerner, Daniel (Ed.) (1972), on "Effective Propaganda: Conditions and Evaluation," in *Propaganda in War and Crisis,* New York: Arno

Lewandowsky, Stephan and John Cook (2020), *The Conspiracy Theory Handbook,*
https://www.climatechangecommunication.org/wp-content/uploads/2020/03/ConspiracyTheoryHandbook.pdf

Lewandowsky, Stephan, Ullrich K.H. Ecker, John Cook, Sander van der Linden, Jon Roozenbeek, and Naomi Oreskes (2023), "Misinformation and the Epistemic Integrity of Democracy," *Current Opinion in Psychology,* 54:101711, Online October 19, pp.1-7,
https://doi.org/10.1016/j.copsyc.2023.101711

Lewandowsky, Stephan, Sander van der Linden, and Andy Norman (2024), "Opinion: Disinformation Is the Real Threat to Democracy and Public Health," *Scientific American,* January 30,
https://www.scientificamerican.com/article/disinformation-is-the-real-threat-to-democracy-and-public-health/

Lewis, Sinclair (2014), *It Can't Happen Here,* New York: Signet [1st published 1935]

Lewis-Kraus, Gideon (2022), "How Harmful is Social Media," *The New Yorker,* June 3,
https://www.newyorker.com/culture/annals-of-inquiry/we-know-less-about-social-media-than-we-think?

Lifton, Robert Jay (1983), *The Protean Self: Human Resilience in an Age of Fragmentation,* New York: Basic Books

Lucas, Edward and Ben Nimmo (2015), "Information Warfare: What Is It and How to Win It?" *Center for European Policy Analysis,* Paper No. 1, November

Mackie, Chris (2016), "Lessons from Ancient Athens: The Art of Exiling Your Enemies," *The Conversation,* November 22,
https://theconversation.com/lessons-from-ancient-athens-the-art-of-exiling-your-enemies-68983

MacLean, Eleanor O'Donnell (1981), *Between the Lines: How to Detect Bias and Propaganda in the News and Everyday Life,* Montreal: Black Rose Books

Madden, Erin (2019) "The Popularization of the Yo-yo," YO-YO–The Mysteries of the Yo-Yo, Fredericksburg, Va.: University of Mary Washington, *WordPress Website,* https://historyoftech.mcclurken.org/yoyo/popularization/the-popularization-of-the-yo-yo

Maddow, Rachel (2023), *Prequel: An American Fight Against Fascism,* Crown: New York

Malkopoulou, Anthoula, Benjamin Moffitt (2023), "How Not to Respond to Populism," *Comparative European Politics,* March 10, https://doi.org/10.1057/s41295-023-00341-9

Mann, Samantha (2019), "Lying and Lie Detection," in Meibauer, Jörg (Ed.), *The Oxford Handbook of Lying,* Oxford: Oxford University Press, pp. 408-419

Mareš, Miroslav and Petra Mlejnková (2021), "Propaganda and Disinformation as a Security Threat," in Gregor, Miloš and Petra Mlejnková (Eds.), *Challenging Online Propaganda and Disinformation in the 21st Century,* Cham, Switzerland: Springer Nature/Palgrave Macmillan, pp. 75-103

Marlin, Randal (1984), "The Rhetoric of Action Description: Ambiguity in Intentional Reference," *Informal Logic,* 6, 3, pp. 26-29, https://doi.org/10.22329/il.v6i3.2737

Marlin, Randal (2013), *Propaganda and the Ethics of Persuasion,* Peterborough, ON: Broadview

Marlin, Randal (2021), "Dynamic Tension for Pandemic Times," *Current Drift,* 10 May, IJES Elul Society, ellul.org/current-drift/dynamic-tension-for-pandemic-times/

Mason, Lance E., Daniel G. Krutka, and Jeremy Stoddard (2018), "Media Literacy, Democracy, and the Challenges of Fake News," *Journal of Media Literacy Education,* 10(2), pp. 1-10, https://digitalcommons.uri.edu/cgi/viewcontent.cgi?article=1389&context=jmle

McCright, A. M. and R. E. Dunlap (2017), "Combatting Misinformation Requires Recognizing Its Types and the Factors That Facilitate Its Spread and Resonance," *Journal of Applied Research in Memory and Cognition,* 6(4), pp. 389-396, https://psycnet.apa.org/doiLanding?doi=10.1016%2Fj.jarmac.2017.09.005

McGee, John A. (1929), *Persuasive Speaking,* New York: Scribner's, pp. 268-269 (Appendix C), https://archive.org/details/persuasivespeaki00mcge

McQuade, Barbara (2024), *Attack from Within: How Disinformation Is Sabotaging America,* New York: Seven Stories Press

Media Education Lab (2024), Harrington School of Communication and Media, University of Rhode Island, mediaeducationlab.com

Michels, Ank and Laurens De Graaf (2017), "Examining Citizen Participation: Local Participatory Policymaking and Democracy Revisited," *Local Government Studies,* 43(6), pp. 875-881, https://www.tandfonline.com/doi/full/10.1080/03003930.2017.1365712

Miller, Rodney G. (2020–2022), Word to the wise blog posts referenced: *It's Time for Plain Talk* 6/25/20, *Pundit Propaganda* 1/13/22, *It's the Propaganda STU**** 9/15/20, *Rip Van Who?* 9/29/2020, *What to Do* 2/24/2021, *Thylacine* 11/1/21, https://communicator.rodney-miller.com

Miller, Rodney G. (2022), *Australians Speak Out: Persuasive Language Styles,* Albany, NY: Parula

Miller, Rodney G. (2023). "Book Review: *A New Semiotics: An Introductory Guide for Students* by David Sless & Ruth Shrensky." *Media International Australia,* Online First, October 6, https://doi.org/10.1177/1329878X231206841

Molina, Maria D., S. Shyam Sundar, Thai Le, and Dongwon Lee (2021), "'Fake News' Is Not Simply False Information: A Concept Explication and Taxonomy of Online Content," *American Behavioral Science,* 65(2), pp. 180-212, https://doi.org/10.1177/0002764219878224

Moral, Pablo, Guillermo Marco, Julio Gonzalo, Jorge Carrillo-de-Albornoz, and Ivan Gonzalo-Verdugo (2023), "Overview of DIPROMATS 2023: Automatic Detection and

Characterization of Propaganda Techniques in Messages from Diplomats and Authorities of World Powers," in Procesamiento del Lenguaje Natural, Revista no 71, Septiembre, pp. 397-407,
https://rua.ua.es/dspace/bitstream/10045/137203/1/PLN_71_31.pdf

Murphy, Dennis M. and James F. White (2007), "Propaganda: Can a Word Decide a War?," *The US Army War College Quarterly: Parameters* 37, 3, pp. 15-27,
https://press.armywarcollege.edu/cgi/viewcontent.cgi?article=2383&context=parameters

Murphy, Gillian, Constance De Saint Laurent, Megan Reynolds, Omar Aftab, Karen Hegarty, Yuning Sun, and Ciara M. Greene (2023), "What Do We Study When We Study Misinformation? A Scoping Review of Experimental Research (2016-2022)," *Harvard Kennedy School Misinformation Review,* November 15,
https://misinforeview.hks.harvard.edu/article/what-do-we-study-when-we-study-misinformation-a-scoping-review-of-experimental-research-2016-2022/

Naffi, Nadia, Melodie Charest, Sarah Danis, Laurie Pique, Ann-Louise Davidson, Nicholas Brault, Marie-Claude Bernard, and Sylivie Barma (2023), "Empowering Youth to Combat Malicious Deepfakes and Disinformation: An Experimental and Reflective Learning Experience Informed by Personal Construct Theory," *Journal of Constructivist Psychology,* December 20,
https://www.tandfonline.com/doi/full/10.1080/10720537.2023.2294314

Neylan, Julian, Mikey Biddlestone, Jon Roozenbeek, and Sander van der Linden (2023), "How to 'Inoculate' against Multimodal Misinformation: A Conceptual Replication of Roozenbeek and Van der Linden (2020), *Scientific Reports,* 13, 18273, https://doi.org/10.1038/s41598-023-43885-2

Oral, Uğur (2023), "'Ostracism,' The People's Way of Protecting Democracy from Tyrants in Ancient Athens," *Electronic Journal of Social Sciences,* April 22, 86, pp. 653-662,
https://dergipark.org.tr/tr/download/article-file/2793784

Orme, Stuart (Director)/Michael Horowitz/IMDbPro (2015), "Trespass," *Foyle's War,* Season 9, Episode 2, https://www.imdb.com/title/tt3474572/

Orwell, George (2009), "Propaganda and Demotic Speech," in Packer, George (Ed.), *All Art is Propaganda,* New York: Mariner, p. 231 [1st published in *Persuasion,* Summer Quarter, 1944, 2, No.2]

Orwell, George (1977), *Animal Farm,* New York: Signet [1st published 1945]

Orwell, George (1981), "Politics and the English Language," *A Collection of Essays,* Orlando, FL: Harcourt, pp. 156-171 [1st published 1946]

Orwell, George (1972), "The Principles of Newspeak," *Nineteen Eighty-Four,* Harmondsworth: Penguin, pp. 241-51 [1st published 1949]

O'Shaughnessy, Nicholas (2017), "Putin, Xi, and Hitler - Propaganda and the Paternity of Pseudo Democracy," *Defense Strategic Communications: The Official Journal of the NATO Strategic Communications Center of Excellence,* 2, Spring, pp. 113-136,
https://stratcomcoe.org/cuploads/pfiles/full_academic_journal_vol2_issuu_07-03-2017.pdf

Packard, Vance (1957), *The Hidden Persuaders,* London: Longmans Green

Paine, Thomas (1997), *Common Sense,* Mineola, NY: Dover, [1st published 1776]

Pamment, James (2020), *The EU's Role in Fighting Disinformation: Taking Back the Initiative,* Carnegie Endowment of International Peace: Washington, DC,
https://www.jstor.org/stable/resrep25788.9

Paul, Christopher and Miriam Matthews (2016), *The Russian "Firehose of Falsehood" Propaganda Model: Why It Might Work and Options to Counter It,* Santa Monica, CA: Rand Corporation, https://www.rand.org/pubs/perspectives/PE198.html

Paul, Christopher and Miriam Matthews (2020), "Defending against Russian Propaganda," in Baines, O'Shaughnessy, and Snow, pp. 286-302

Petelin, Roslyn (2014), *UQx Write101x English Grammar and Style*-Video, St. Lucia, Qld: The University of Queensland, *Website*,
https://www.youtube.com/channel/UC8qZTqvQsFomCo6xFNX7GZg

Phillips, Whitney (2019), "It Wasn't Just the Trolls: Early Internet Culture, 'Fun,' and the Fires of Exclusionary Laughter," *Social Media + Society*, pp. 1-4,
https://journals.sagepub.com/doi/pdf/10.1177/2056305119849493

Pinker, Steven (2006), "Block That Metaphor!" *The New Republic*, October 8,
https://newrepublic.com/article/77730/block-metaphor-steven-pinker-whose-freedom-george-lakoff

Piskorska, Galyna, Daria Ryzhova, and Anatoly Yakovets (2023), "Joint Efforts of the Media, Civil Society, and the State to Counter Russian Disinformation," *International Journal of Innovative Technologies in Social Science*, 3(39),
https://www.researchgate.net/publication/373232700_JOINT_EFFORTS_OF_THE_MEDIA_CIVIL_SOCIETY_AND_THE_STATE_TO_COUNTER_RUSSIAN_DISINFORMATION

Podemska, Justyna and Piotr Podemski, (2023), "Protect Yourself Against Disinformation," in Kupiecki, Robert and Agnieszka Legucka (Eds.), *Disinformation and the Resilience of Democratic Societies*, Warsaw: Polski Institute Spraw Międzynarodowych, pp. 265-285,
https://www.researchgate.net/publication/372419503_Disinformation_and_the_Resilience_of_Democratic_Societies

Pomerantsev, Peter (2019), *This is NOT Propaganda: Adventures in the War Against Reality*, London: Faber and Faber

Pradelle, Alexaine, Sabine Mainbourg, Steeve Provencher, Emmanuel Massy, Guillaume Grenet, Jean-Christophe Lega (2024), "Deaths Induced by Compassionate Use of Hydroxychloroquine during the First COVID-19 Wave: An Estimate," *Biomedicine & Pharamacotherapy*, 171, Online January 2,
https://www.sciencedirect.com/science/article/pii/S075333222301853X

Ratcliffe, Susan (2010), *Oxford Dictionary of Quotations by Subject*, Oxford: Oxford University Press

Ressa, Maria (2022), *How to Stand Up to a Dictator: The Fight for Our Future*, New York: Harper

Ridge, Hannah M. (2023), "The d-word: Surveying Democracy in America," *Democratization*,
https://doi.org/10.1080/13510347.2023.2284279

Robinson, Viviane, Frauke Meyer, Deidre Le Fevre, and Claire Sinnema (n.d.), "The Quality of Leaders's Problem-solving Conversations: Truth-seeking or Truth-claiming?"
https://researchspace.auckland.ac.nz/bitstream/handle/2292/56563/Robinson%20et%20al%20(2020)%20truth-seeking_author%20copy.pdf?sequence=1

Roozenbeek, Jon, Eileen Culloty, and Jane Suiter (2022), "Countering Misinformation: Evidence, Knowledge Gaps, and Implications of Current Interventions," *European Psychologist*, 28(3), pp.189-205, published online July 14, 2023,
https://econtent.hogrefe.com/doi/full/10.1027/1016-9040/a000492

Rosenberg, Justus (2020), *The Art of Resistance: My Four Years in the French Underground, a Memoir*, New York: Harper Collins

Ruffo, Giancario Alfonso Semeraro, Anastasia Giachanou, Paolo Rosso (2023), "Studying Fake News Spreading, Polarisation Dynamics, and Manipulation by Bots: A Tale of Networks and Language," *Computer Science Review*, 47, February,
https://doi.org/10.1016/j.cosrev.2022.100531

Russell, Bertrand (1976), *The Impact of Science on Society,* London: Unwin [1st edition, 1952]

Salaverría, Ramón and Gustavo Cardoso (2023), "Future of Disinformation Studies: Emerging Research Fields," *Professional de la Información,* 32(5), e320525, pp. 1-7, https://doi.org/10.3145/epi.2023.sep.25

Sanderson III, Paul G. (2009), *Augustus Saint-Gaudens: Master of American Sculpture,* PBS Documentary, Our Town Films, WNET/Thirteen, September 13, https://www.youtube.com/watch?v=8t8K7Aisx8U

Sayers, Dorothy L. (1948), *The Lost Tools of Learning: Paper Read at a Vacation Course in Education, Oxford, 1947,* London: Methuen

Schiffrin, Anya (2018), "Fighting Disinformation with Media Literacy–in 1939," *Columbia Journalism Review,* October 10, https://www.cjr.org/innovations/institute-propaganda-analysis.php

Schiffrin, Anya (2022), "Fighting Disinformation in the 1930s: Clyde Miller and the Institute for Propaganda Analysis," *International Journal of Communication,* 16, pp. 3715-3741, https://ijoc.org/index.php/ijoc/article/viewFile/17931/3848

Schleifer, Ron (2020), "Countering Hamas and Hezbollah Propaganda," in Baines, O'Shaughnessy, and Snow, pp. 272-285

Shaffer, Kris (2019), *Data Versus Democracy: How Big Data Algorithms Shape Opinions and Alter the Course of History,* New York: Apress/Springer Science + Business Media

Silina, Maria (2022), "Russia's Feminists Are Protesting the War and Its Propaganda with Stickers, Posters, Performance and Graffiti," *The Conversation,* April 7, https://theconversation.com/russias-feminists-are-protesting-the-war-and-its-propaganda-with-stickers-posters-performance-and-graffiti-179989

Simchon, Almog, Matthew Edwards, and Stephan Lewandowsky (2024), "The Persuasive Effects of Political Microtargeting in the Age of Generative AI," *PNAS Nexus,* January 29, p. 35, https://doi.org/10.1093/pnasnexus/pgae035, quoting House of Commons, U.K. Parliament (2019), *Digital, Culture, Media and Sport Committee, Disinformation and "fake news:" Final Report,* Technical Report

Sless, David and Ruth Shresky (2023), *A New Semiotics: An Introductory Guide for Students,* London and New York: Routledge

Smith, Zhanna Malekos (2020), "Part II: How the Information Environment is Testing the Mettle of Liberal Democracies," in *Burnt by the Digital Sun,* Washington, DC: Center for Strategic and International Studies, pp. 9-16, https://www.jstor.org/stable/resrep25686.7

Snow, Nancy (2007), "Media, Terrorism, and the Politics of Fear," *Media Development,* 3, pp. 17-22, https://www.researchgate.net/publication/288936034_Media_terrorism_and_the_politics_of_fear

Snow, Nancy (2013), *Truth Is the Best Propaganda: Edward R. Murrow's Speeches in the Kennedy Years,* Minerva, NY: Minerva Press

Snow, Nancy (2020), *Unmasking the Virus: Public Diplomacy and the Pandemic,* Public Diplomacy Council, the Public Diplomacy Association of America, and the USC Annenberg Center for Communications Leadership & Policy, June 9, https://www.youtube.com/watch?v=v6jA_JaSefc

Snow, Nancy E. (Ed.) (2024), *The Self, Civic Virtue, and Public Life,* Abingdon: Routledge, https://library.oapen.org/bitstream/handle/20.500.12657/87406/1/9781040016800.pdf

Snyder, Timothy (2017), *On Tyranny: Twenty Lessons from the Twentieth Century*, New York: Tim Duggan

Sproule, J. Michael (1994), *Channels of Propaganda*, Bloomington, IN: EDINFO Press and ERIC Clearinghouse

Sproule, J. Michael (1997), *Propaganda and Democracy: The American Experience of Media and Mass Persuasion*, Cambridge: Cambridge University Press

Sproule, J. Michael (2001), "Authorship and Origins of the Seven Propaganda Devices: A Research Note," *Rhetoric and Public Affairs*, 4(1), Spring, pp. 135-143

Sproule, J. Michael (2020), *Democratic Vernaculars: Rhetorics of Reading, Writing, Speaking, and Criticism since the Enlightenment*, New York: Routledge

Srour, Camille and Jacques Py (2023), "The General Theory of Deception: A Disruptive Theory of Lie Production, Prevention, and Detection," *Psychological Review*, 130(5), pp. 1289-1309, https://psycnet.apa.org/fulltext/2022-92735-001.pdf

Stanley, Jason (2015), *How Propaganda Works*, Princeton: Princeton University Press

Steinfatt, Thomas M. (1979), "Evaluating Approaches to Propaganda Analysis," *ETC: A Review of General Semantics*, 36(2), Summer, pp. 157-180

Tannenbaum, Melanie B., Justin Hepler, Rick S. Zimmerman, Lindsey Saul, Samantha Jacobs, Kristina Wilson, and Delores Albarracín (2015), "Appealing to Fear: A Meta-Analysis of Fear Appeal Effectiveness and Theories," *Psychological Bulletin*, 141(6), pp. 1178-1204, https://www.apa.org/pubs/journals/releases/bul-a0039729.pdf

Taylor, P. M. (2002), "Strategic Communications or Democratic Propaganda?" *Journalism Studies*, 3, 3, pp. 437-441, https://doi.org/10.1080/14616700220145641

Teperik, Dmitri, Solvita Denisa-Liepniece, Dalia Bankauskaitė, and Kaarel Kullamaa (2022), *Resilience Against Disinformation: A New Baltic Way to Follow?* Estonia: International Centre for Defence and Security, https://icds.ee/en/resilience-against-disinformation-a-new-baltic-way-to-follow/ and https://www.researchgate.net/publication/364474732_Resilience_Against_Disinformation_A_New_Baltic_Way_to_Follow

Teubert, Wolfgang (2019), "The Citizen Caught Between Dialogue, Bureaucracy," in Paige, Ruth, Beatrix Busse and Nina Nørgaard (Eds.), *Rethinking Language, Text and Context: Interdisciplinary Research in Stylistics in Honour of Michael Toolan*, Abingdon: Routledge, pp. 303-320

Tsipursky, G. (2017), "Towards a Post-lies Future: Fighting 'Alternative Facts' and 'Post-truth' Politics," *The Humanist*, 77(2), pp. 12-15, https://www.proquest.com/docview/1873942879?pq-origsite=gscholar&fromopenview=true&sourcetype=Magazines

Toler, Aric (2017), "Most Common Way that Fake News Spreads Is from Laziness," STOPFAKE.ORG, www.stopfake.org

Tripodi, Francesca Bolla (2022), *The Propagandist's Playbook: How Conservative Elites Manipulate Search and Threaten Democracy*, New Haven: Yale University Press

Turnbull, Nick (2017), "Political Rhetoric and Its Relationship to Context: A New Theory of the Rhetorical Situations, the Rhetorical and the Political," *Critical Discourse Studies*, XXX, pp. 115-1131

United Nations (1948), *Universal Declaration of Human Rights*, Article 3

United States Census Bureau (2023), *At Height of Pandemic, More Than 51% of People Age 16 and Over Helped Neighbors, More Than 23% Formally Volunteered*, January 25, https://www.census.gov/library/stories/2023/01/volunteering-and-civic-life-in-america.html

Van der Linden, Sander (2023), *Foolproof: Why Misinformation Infects Our Minds and How to Build Immunity,* New York: W.W. Norton

Ventsel, Andreas, Sten Hansson, Merit Rickberg, and Mari-Liis Madisson (2023), "Building Resilience against Hostile Information Influence Activities: How a New Media Literacy Learning Platform Was Developed for the Estonian Defense Forces," *Armed Forces and Society,* April 18, pp. 1-21, https://journals.sagepub.com/doi/full/10.1177/0095327X231163265?af=R&ai=1gvoi&mi=3ricys

Wanless, Alicia and Michael Berk (2020), "Audience Is the Amplifier: Participatory Propaganda," in Baines, O'Shaughnessy, and Snow, pp. 85-104

Wanless, Alicia and Michael Berk (2022), "Participatory Propaganda: The Engagement of Audiences in the Spread of Persuasive Communications," in Herbert, David and Stefan Fisher (Eds.), *Social Media and Social Order,* De Gruyter Open Poland, doi.org/10.2478/9788366675612-009

Weigle, Michelle C. (2023), "The Use of Web Archives in Disinformation Research," *arXiv.org,* June, https://arxiv.org/abs/2306.10004

Weimann, Gabriel (2020), "The Evolution of Terrorist Propaganda in Cyberspace," in Baines, O'Shaughnessy, and Snow, pp. 577-592

Wilson, Anna, Seb Wilkes, Yayoi Teramoto, and Scott Hale (2023), "Multimodal Analysis of Disinformation and Misinformation," *Royal Society Open Science,* 10: 230964, https://doi.org/10.1098/rsos.230964

Wilson, Douglas L. (2007), *Lincoln's Sword: The Presidency and the Power of Words,* New York: Vintage

Winter, Charlie and Craig Whiteside (2020), "IS's Strategic Communication Tactics," in Baines, O'Shaughnessy, and Snow, pp. 566-576

Wollaeger, Mark (2013), "Propaganda and Pleasure: From Kracauer to Joyce," in Auerbach, Johathan and Russ Castronovo (Eds.), *The Oxford Handbook of Propaganda Studies,* New York: Oxford University Press, pp. 278-297

Wood, Tim (2021), "Propaganda, Obviously: How Propaganda Analysis Fixates on the Hidden and Misses the Conspicuous," *Harvard Kennedy School Misinformation Review,* 2(1), April 8, https://misinforeview.hks.harvard.edu/article/propaganda-obviously-how-propaganda-analysis-fixates-on-the-hidden-and-misses-the-conspicuous/

Woolley, Samuel C. and Howard, Philip N. (2019), *Computational Propaganda: Political Parties, Politicians and Political Manipulation on Social Media,* Oxford: Oxford University Press

Young, Marilyn J., Michael K. Launer, and Curtis C. Austin (1990), "The Need for Evaluative Criteria: Conspiracy Argument Revisited, Argumentation and Advocacy," 26(3), pp. 89-107, https://www.researchgate.net/publication/321897158_The_Need_for_Evaluative_Criteria_Conspiracy_Argument_Revisited

Zada, John (2021), *Veils of Distortion: How the News Media Warps Our Minds,* Toronto: Terra Incognita

Zamęcki, Łukasz and Adam Szymański (2023), "Unintentional Democratic Backsliders. 'Evil Always Wins through the Strength of Its Splendid Dupes,'" *Polish Political Science Review,* 11(1), June 30, pp. 40-41, https://sciendo.com/article/10.2478/ppsr-2023-0003

Ziemer, Carolin-Theresa and Tobias Rothmund (2024), "Psychological Underpinnings of Misinformation Countermeasures," *Journal of Media Psychology,* January 23, https://econtent.hogrefe.com/doi/10.1027/1864-1105/a000407

ACKNOWLEDGMENTS

My thanks go to all who "do something" to strengthen democracy. With special acknowledgment to readers of the blog, I appreciate your encouraging responses to what we feel are important concerns. I am also grateful to many writers, other thoughtful commentators, colleagues, friends, former teachers, and family members who continuously help shape my thinking, daily living, and writing. Thank you for your insights, kindness, and humor. Finally, for my wife's generosity, good sense, talents, and love, I am forever most grateful.

INDEX

A

ABCs (of IPA), 43
accountability, 7, 26-28, 70
    delay, 31, 35
Achilles heel, 52
acquiescence, 54, 61
adverbs, 20
Aesop, 19
agenda, public, 12, 18, 24, 30, 34
Alexander the Great, 32
ambiguity, 15, 17- 21, 58
American Revolutionary War, 69
amphiboly, 43
analogy, 10, 19, 23, 61
    false, 43
Animal Farm, 15
anti-democracy, vi, 23, 36-38, 56, 70
    populism, 31
    rule, 32
artificial intelligence, 6
Athens, 53
attorney, 22
attorneys-general, 50
audience, vi, 6, 13, 20, 24
    action, 21, 47
    analysts, 42, 66
    emotions, 55
    members, 20, 42
    of media, 27, 58-59
    pre-exposure of, 40
    reach, 18
    solutions for, 2, 12, 23, 27, 44, 60, 68
Augustus, 32
autocracy, 1-4, 60-61
autocrat, 1-2, 27, 30, 32, 34, 37
    aspiring/wannabe, 9, 16, 49, 73
    pigs, 15
    propagandist, 25, 39-40, 51-54
    "tells," 34-35

B

babysitter, electronic, 14
backsliding, democratic, 49
bait, 19, 27, 36
behavior, 13, 28, 57-58
    automatic, 16, 67
    contrarian, 56
    corrupt, 10

illegal/illicit, 22, 27
"big lie," 18, 37
bluff, 31, 35
boosting, 32
    as intervention, 46
Boy Who Cried Wolf, 19
brainwashing, 75
breaking news, 11, 38, 59
bribe, 30
broadcast, 11, 26, 56, 65
broadcaster, 11
    moderation of, 58, 66
bully, 19

C

campaign, 21, 50, 55
    election, 24, 40, 41
    propaganda, 42
Camus, Albert, 5
Capitol, 22
celebrity, 11, 18, 59
censorship, 7, 52
    self-, 54
century
    eighteenth, 5, 32-33, 47
    twentieth, 32, 44-45
    twenty-first, 69
certainty, 17-20, 31
character assassination, 23, 27, 42
characterizations, 19
charlatan, 31, 65
circus, 59, 65
civics, 45, 51
civic leaders, 14, 25, 28, 39, 50-52, 60
civic virtues, 55
civility, 6, 27, 31, 37
civilizations, 32
Chomsky, Noam, 17, 33
coalition, 9, 23, 24, 61
coercion, 30, 32, 36, 54
Collins, Philip, 19-20, 34
Common Sense, 1,
communication, 41, 55, 64
    channels, 21, 37-38, 40, 70
    digital, 21, 44, 46, 47
community, 2
    democratic, 33
    engagement, 25, 45, 49, 60

105

I

identity, 1, 19
    national, 12
indoctrination, 63
inoculation, psychological, 40, 46
ideology, 24, 46
Iklé, Fred, 18
Independent, 23
institutions, 7, 10, 16, 20, 22, 36-37
    zones of comfort in, 49
intelligence, 30-31
intent, vi, 11, 52
intention, 12-13, 19, 24, 42, 46, 55
Institute for Propaganda Analysis (IPA), 43
    devices, 43-44
    ABCs, 43
Internet, vi, 27, 37, 44, 50, 54
intimidation, 2, 31, 36
-ism, 11, 52
It Can't Happen Here, v

J

job, 7, 24, 28, 38, 56, 64, 70
    description, 49
journalism, 2, 25-26, 58-59
    constructive, 27
    investigative, 27
journalist, 8, 19, 22, 25-26, 33, 39, 49, 58-59
Jowett, Garth S., 13
judge, 39, 49-50
judiciary, 7, 9, 22, 52, 57, 60
juggernaut, 52, 58
justice, 27, 28, 29, 36, 70
    denied, 50

K

King of England, 1
King James I, 48
knowledge, 17

L

labeling, 46
Larson, Gary, 71
law, 2, 6, 27, 29, 73
    addressing lies, 44, 51-52
    electoral, 52
    gaming of, 27, 39, 50
    reform, 41, 52, 58
    remedies at, 42

    rule of, 22, 46
    undermining of, 31, 36, 49
lawyer, 39, 61, 73
leaders, civic, 14, 25, 28, 39, 50-52, 60
legislator, 7, 39, 50, 57
Lewis, Sinclair, v
liberty, 5, 7, 16, 36, 55
lie, 6-8, 14, 23, 28, 32, 42
    call out, 31, 41, 55, 61
    "big," 18, 37
    Illegality of, 51-52
    media role, 58
    outrageous, 57
    spotting, 44
Lincoln, Abraham, 59
linguist, 17, 20
literacy
    community, 45, 49
    information, 46
    media, 45, 46
lying, 52

M

MacLean, Eleanor, 43
Marlboro Man, 6
Marlin, Randal, 13, 19, 31-32, 43
Mather, Kirtley, 43
McGee, Sandra, 45
media
    change, 58-60
    exposé, 57
    literacy, 45, 46
    mass, 3, 6, 8, 9, 11, 18, 26, 41, 46
    release, 38, 56
    social, 2, 3, 6, 12, 14, 19, 37, 46, 47, 69, 75
memory, 15
menace, 13, 23, 40
metaphor, 17
microtargeting, vi, 39
Miller, Clyde R, 43
misinformation, vi
    and appeals, 16
    counter, 23, 56
    and democracy, 5-6
    digital detection, 44
    gold standard, 4
    research, 46

Montesquieu, 7
murder, 14
myth, 12, 14, 16-17, 32, 54
  of utopia, 34, 37, 38
N
name, 19, 23, 25, 39, 64
  -recognition, 34
name-calling, 19, 43
national debt, 68
national identity, 12, 28
national narrative, 17
national security, 37
Nazis, 65
Newspeak, 11, 15, 63
1930s, 33
Nineteen Eighty-Four, 15
Nobel Peace Prize, 2
norm, 6, 15, 20, 31, 56, 67
  democratic, 22
  nudge, 46
  reappraisal of, 34-35
novelty, 7, 20, 45
O
O'Donnell, Victoria, 13, 41
Orwell, George, 10, 14-15, 63, 67, 70, 74
O'Shaughnessy, Nicholas, 54
ostracism, 53
outrage, 3, 11, 58
  amplifying, 6, 39, 65
  claims, 20
  of dupes, 30
  ignoring, 68
  manufactured, 10, 16, 26
P
Paine, Thomas, 1,
parasite, 10
"party faithful," 24
party line, 42
party whip, 33
persuasion, 12, 31, 45, 46
  campaigns, 55
Philippines, 2, 61
pillars, 2, 49
plausible, 15, 54, 57
polemic, 22, 41, 58, 60
  types, 25

postal service, 37, 70
prebunking, 30, 34, 40, 46, 56
pre-exposing, 40
pre-propaganda, 33-35
profiling, psychographic, 27
Propaganda, 41
propaganda, vi, 12
  ancient, 32
  anti-democratic, 23, 36, 38, 56
  antidote, 15, 40
  autocratic, 3-4, 25, 30, 32, 51, 54, 61
  boost, 24, 32
  computerized, 6, 39
  and cyberspace, 46
  of deed, 6, 14, 30, 46
  defined, 11-14
  democratic, 31-32, 33
  devices, 42-43
  domestic, 72-74
  durability 24
  education, 7, 8, 44-46
  on public agenda, 12, 18, 24, 30, 34
  firehose of, 6, 40, 41
  Hamas, 46
  Hezbollah, 46
  harm, 3, 6, 10, 14
  ideological perspective, 24, 46
  limits of, 27-28
  Orwell on, 10
  pre-propaganda, 33-35
  process, 17-21
  Russian, 46
  social, 67
  "tells of," 34, 37, 70
  terrorist, 3, 46, 56, 72-74
  types of, 35-36
Propaganda & Persuasion, 41
proximity, 20
pseudo-populism, vi, 2, 4, 6, 16, 23, 60
public, 33, 38, 43, 48, 59
public opinion, 47
puerile, 67
puffery, 12, 25, 52
pundit, 8, 14, 19, 25, 39, 51, 59, 65-67
Q
quality of life, 10
question, direct, 24

108

109

www.ingramcontent.com/pod-product-compliance
Lightning Source LLC
Chambersburg PA
CBHW031130020426
42333CB00012B/307